The Rocking Chair Reader

Family Gatherings

True Stories of Celebration and Reunion

Edited by Helen Kay Polaski

Adams Media
Avon, Massachusetts

Published by
Adams Media, an F+W Publications Company
57 Littlefield Street, Avon, MA 02322. U.S.A.
www.adamsmedia.com and *www.rockingchairreader.com*

ISBN: 1-59337-348-1

Printed in the United States of America.

J I H G F E D C B A

Library of Congress Cataloging-in-Publication Data
Available from Publisher

This publication is designed to provide accurate and authoritative information with regard
to the subject matter covered. It is sold with the understanding that the publisher is not
engaged in rendering legal, accounting, or other professional advice. If legal advice or
other expert assistance is required, the services of a competent professional person should
be sought.
—From a *Declaration of Principles* jointly adopted by a Committee of the
American Bar Association and a Committee of Publishers and Associations

Many of the designations used by manufacturers and sellers to distinguish their products
are claimed as trademarks. Where those designations appear in this book and Adams
Media was aware of a trademark claim, the designations have been printed with initial
capital letters.

Interior illustrations by Roberta A. Ridolfi.
Interior textures copyright ©2002 Marlin Studios.

This book is available at quantity discounts for bulk purchases.
For information, call 1-800-872-5627.

This book is dedicated to
families everywhere, but most
importantly to the family of
Harry and Stella Szymanski
of Metz, Michigan.
May each of us continue to realize
the importance of family
and prioritize accordingly.

Contents

◄○►

Acknowledgments

As I sit down to write this passage, I suddenly feel inadequate. There are so many who deserve to be acknowledged.

Without the Lord on my side, I wouldn't have gotten anywhere. Without my agent, Deirdre Mullane, I wouldn't have found Adams Media. Without Adams Media, I wouldn't have discovered *The Rocking Chair Reader* series, and without this series I would never have met and worked with all of the wonderful authors who are as much a part of this series as I am, nor would I have met any of the wonderful people at Adams Media who definitely keep it all afloat. And, of course, without my readers, I would be nowhere.

I feel very privileged to have read each of the stories that came my way as this book progressed, and I thank every one of the authors for sharing of themselves so thoroughly. By telling the intimate and precious stories from your personal family gatherings, you help others to recall their own stories. It is my hope that when your story is read, you will become instrumental in helping those who may have forgotten the true meaning of family and its importance in their lives, and perhaps help them find their way back to happier times.

◄○►

As I worked on this book, my own loved ones kept me on task, for they, better than anyone, show me what family gatherings are all about. Had I been given the opportunity to choose my own family, rest assured I would have chosen each one of you.

Creating profiles on select towns in the book required a special kind of dedication, and each person who helped me on this project deserves a special kind of thanks. I would not have found the wonderful flavor of each of these ten towns without the research assistance from the following individuals:

John R. Bradley (Hendersonville, Tennessee)

Ray Heyden Burson (Doniphan, Missouri)

Candy Killion (Verona, New Jersey)

Galen Pittman and Culver Heater, Jr. (Glendora, California)

Jonita Mullins, Marketing Director at Three Rivers Museum (Muskogee, Oklahoma)

Amy O'Quinn, Edward and Betty McIntyre, Carroll and Bettye Singletary, Faye Vickers, and DeLois Handley (Irwinville, Georgia)

Rachael Phillips and the Jackson Parish Library (Eros, Louisiana)

Dorothy Read, Margery Gilde, Nellie Assink, and Mike Siebold (Gleed, Washington)

Mary Helen Straker (Whigville, Ohio)

Gayle Sorensen Stringer (Tyler, Minnesota)

Thank you one and all. My heart sings whenever I think of how we all came together on this one project, each pulling equally hard, to create, once again, a masterpiece.

Introduction

FAMILY IS EVERYTHING TO ME. I can't think of a better way to spend my time than in the company of my family—any one of my kin or all of them at the same time. I love being together with them, and I love listening to their individual stories and sharing mine with them. I love the unconditional acceptance that surrounds the family nucleus and I hold tightly to the prospect of keeping that unit strong.

I look forward to family gatherings like a child looks forward to Christmas. I count the days until each one, telephoning my sisters endlessly to see what dish everyone is bringing, find out what everyone is wearing, discuss what activities we'll be involved in, and to relive the fun times we had the last time we were together.

Birthdays, baptisms, weddings, holidays, surprise parties, picnics—you name it, I love it. But perhaps the most enjoyable gatherings are those that take place on the spur of the moment. Last weekend was a perfect example. My baby sister and artist, Melissa Jane (Szymanski) Mau, was having an art show less than thirty minutes from where I was holding a book signing. Both of these events were about an hour from where our sister, Veronica Joan Dickerson, lives. It was an opportunity not to be missed! Roni and I met and snapped photos of Missy's artwork, her first-place ribbon, and the mile-wide smile that never left her face. Then we enjoyed lunch—a half hour of reminiscing and sharing what was on our plates as well as what had happened in our individual lives since two weeks before, when we three had last met. For the first twenty minutes of my book signing, my two sisters sat nearby, supporting me with their presence and snapping photos for posterity. Then I shooed them off to enjoy an afternoon of shopping while I took care of business. Afterward, we went shopping together, shared photos taken at the last gathering—and laughed until our sides hurt and our lips were curled into permanent smiles.

My sisters and I talked about everything under the sun, including our upcoming adventures. In two weeks, eight sisters and four nieces would be traveling to Chicago for a long weekend. We tell the rest of the world that it's a necessary Christmas shopping spree—but it isn't. It's just to keep the channels open, to be near one another, and to feel that closeness once again. We're family, and each of us knows that these ties are the ones you never want to break.

That feeling—that very same sense of bonding—is exactly what we hope this book will bring to readers. My authors recognize the importance of family and have shared some of their most special moments with the rest of us. These stories are easy on the eyes and ears, and so very important to the heart. I feel confident that you will enjoy them as much as I do. Thank you once again for joining us and becoming part of *The Rocking Chair Reader* family.

Helen Kay Polaski

One of the Family

by T. Suzanne Eller | *Muskogee, Oklahoma*

IT ALL STARTED OUT ON A WHIM. I recklessly perched in the window of the 1969 mint-green Mustang, waving as we sped down the streets of the small college town. I was a city girl in a country town.

We pulled into a fast-food restaurant, a local hangout, and a car followed. Two college-age boys climbed out—obviously country, both in blue jeans and cowboy boots. One boldly stared, then smiled. I felt the crimson flush of embarrassment climb up my neck and my heart took a leap. I fell in love that night before he even spoke a word. He said he fell in love with me when he saw my brown hair flying in the wind.

He was the first farmer I had ever met and I was the first city girl he had ever dated. He was a third-generation dairy farmer, he explained. Of course, I said I knew where milk came from—you picked it up at Safeway, right? He laughed, not understanding that I was only half-kidding.

After dating for several weeks, he wanted me to join him to meet his family. As we traveled down Highway 69, he told me to look for the "Y" in the road. He laughed when I told him I didn't see a YMCA anywhere on the horizon. He laughed harder when he realized I was serious.

We approached a small school, nestled in the heart of a big, wide-open, and very green countryside. When he drove into the parking lot, I looked at him in surprise. "I thought I was meeting your family," I said.

"You are," he replied. Then he grabbed me by the hand and walked through the doors of the Oktaha gymnasium as if it were his home.

The aroma of homemade gravy filled the air. There was more food laid out on the long brown school tables than I had ever seen. Tubs of mashed potatoes with real butter. Pies of every variety— every crust homemade and crimped with expertise.

The huge room was filled with people, who stood in close, inti-mate groups laughing and talking. I turned to him in confusion. "I thought I was meeting your family."

"You are," he replied. "This is my family."

I stared at the crowd of people as they came toward me, wel-coming me. They already knew my name. I knew none of theirs.

Nearby, an elderly man and woman sat on a piano bench. She was large-boned and pretty, with soft blue eyes and a tentative smile. The old man tapped his feet in rhythm with the music playing on the school piano. His skin was dark, worn, and smooth. He wore a white shirt and overalls. They were the parents of eleven children—six girls and five boys. The room held the children, grandchildren, and great-grandchildren of this couple.

I stared in disbelief. There were five of us in my family. Once a year we visited grandparents who were virtually strangers.

I watched in amazement as more people—and food—came through the door. In addition to ham and turkey, fifty-plus bowls of vegetables, salads, and side dishes were visible. But the highlight was to come: the desserts. Chocolate pies and chocolate cakes; apple cobbler; and lemon meringue, apple, cherry, blueberry, pineapple, coconut cream, strawberry, and pecan pies.

Around us, kids played ball, roller-skated, and hollered. But the noise from the kids didn't come close to the noise generated by the adults. I thought of my quiet family—no talking at the dinner table. These people laughed, danced, and played at the dinner table.

A pretty young woman nearby captivated her audience. She laughed wildly, gesturing with manicured hands. The older women around her collapsed into laughter. One leaned against the wall, tears streaming down her face, "Quit girl, you're killing me," she cried. Another woman squeezed her legs together, running to the bathroom, which only caused further hilarity.

Blue jeans and overalls with white, starched shirts held the day. Every man wore boots. The men were tall and carried their wives' good cooking around their middle.

One tall, dark-haired man held court in a corner of the room. A toothpick dangled from the corner of his mouth, bouncing as he told a story. The other men laughed with this one—my father-in-law-to-be. As the light caught his features, I gasped, seeing a younger face of the elderly grandfather and, for a brief moment, my love's face as well. So many generations in one room. How would I ever fit into all of this?

As of this past Thanksgiving, I have now been part of that family, the Ellers, for twenty-five years. And again for this holiday, a group of more than 200 family members met in the same small rural school cafeteria. Grandma and Grandpa are gone. One of the laughing aunts has joined them.

The best part of being an Eller is that I found a small-town treasure I never knew existed. I am now part of a large, close-knit family. There have been good times and hard times. I've made mistakes adjusting to a large family, but I worked through those mistakes and came out stronger because of them.

For instance, I learned that if you want something to remain secret, you keep it to yourself, because this family is a small community. I learned that if I wanted something, I had to open my mouth. I also learned what it was like to have a family surround you when you find out you have cancer at thirty-two years of age, and to dance with you when you beat it. I learned the value of family—something my own kids take for granted, but I love that they do. It's something they've always had, something they count on, rest in, and look forward to when they come home from college.

On this holiday, I set my brownies from a box mix on the table and smile. I can't compete with the homemade crusts and don't even try. As I glance at the door, I see my college-age son lead a young woman through the door. I am captivated as I recognize the look on her face. She looks stricken, and I hear her say, "I thought you were bringing me to meet your family."

"This is my family," he replies, squeezing her hand in reassurance.

I quickly walk toward her, my arms open. The rest of the family follows. We already know her name.⊷

Muskogee, Oklahoma

Population: 38,000

Town Facts

Incorporated • Muskogee began as a railhead in 1872, but did not incorporate until April 1898. (Towns with no Native American residents were called "Non-Indian" towns and they could not incorporate in Indian Territory until the Curtis Act of 1898.)

Original names • Muscogee was the original spelling of the town, named after the Muscogee (Creek) tribe of Native Americans. The spelling was changed to Muskogee in 1900.

Location • Muskogee is located in northeastern Oklahoma, at the conjunction of the Arkansas, Grand, and Verdigris rivers. It is 50 miles southeast of Tulsa, and about 110 miles east of Oklahoma City, the state capital. Muskogee lies at the edge of the foothills of the Ozark Mountains.

Industry and transportation • Georgia Pacific, a paper mill, is Muskogee's largest employer. The second largest employers are two regional hospitals. Muskogee has a number of small manufacturing plants and is home to a regional office of the Veterans Administration. Transportation plays a large part in the town's economy: Muskogee is located on Highway 69, a major north-south corridor, and on the Union Pacific Railroad. Also a port city, Muskogee has one of the furthermost inland ports in America with barge traffic hauling steel, wheat, and coal.

The Ellers of Muscogee

Suzanne Eller (Suzie) writes, "with over 200 family members in Muskogee County, the Eller family has remained close though generations and family ties have multiplied. 'Once an Eller, always an Eller' is a favorite saying. That is because it's more than a last name. It's belonging.

It's getting together at holidays. It's attending baby showers a
and pulling in tight when tragedy hits. It's knowing who you
the last person in your family who carried the Eller name was yo
grandmother. It's something my children have always had and p
sometimes take for granted. But it's something I will always love!" ∾

Interesting People

uskogee has been home to doctors, lawyers, and Native American chiefs, including General Pleasant Porter, chief of the
Muscogee tribe; Charles N. Haskell, Oklahoma's first governor; Alice Rob-
ertson, Oklahoma's first and only congresswoman; and U.S. marshals Leo
Bennett, Bud Ledbetter, and Bass Reeves, the first African-American in
American history to serve as a deputy marshal. In the 1930s Muskogee produced such jazz greats as Jay McShann, Don Byas, and Barney Kessel. ∾

Interesting Facts

e cause it sits at the confluence of three navigable rivers, the region
around Muskogee was one of the first to be settled and developed
in what later became known as Oklahoma. This spot was also a lucrative fur
trading area between the European traders and Native Americans. When
the United States government placed southeastern tribes on Indian Territory, the Cherokees and Creeks settled in the Three Rivers area. Muskogee
was born on the M-K-T rail line, the first railroad to cross Indian Territory
in 1872. Because of its accessible location, the federal government chose
Muskogee to be its seat of administration in Indian Territory. The Union
Agency to the Five Civilized Tribes, the territory's first federal court, and
the Congressional Dawes Commission were all located in Muskogee. At
one time, Muskogee had more federal employees than any other town except Washington, D.C. ∾

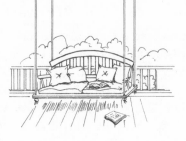

THIS BOG WAS SMALLER THAN THE OTHERS. Not much more than a dozen acres, but it was dense with the fattest, tastiest blueberries I'd ever picked. It was framed awkwardly in the tall, dark trees of the New Jersey Pine Barrens, which surrounded the bushes on all sides and cast a mixture of wraithlike shadows and radiant sunlight over the deep-set field. The bog's boundaries were uneven and crooked, the dams built many years before.

It was the summer of my thirteenth year. My three brothers and I had come up from Moorestown a week earlier, as we did every year, to help Uncle Zach with the summer harvest. My fingers were already stained blue with berry wax from collecting 100 pounds a day.

My grandfather, who'd worked the same fields for sixty years, watched us work and helped when he could, though he often just played his guitar. We slept on the porch each night with half a dozen other cousins. We ate our aunts' various deep-dish cobblers and played penny poker until the first whippoorwill hoot.

Uncle Zach managed four bogs just outside of Chatsworth, and I'd worked in each along with the early July crew for the past five years. It's a wonderful memory now, but at the time, I wasn't there by choice. In fact, I'd even argued against it, but Mother made me go. She said her brother needed our help to get by each year. So here I was again, a few miles west of Uncle Zach's home, in a new bog.

We took the trucks to get there each day, moving through the shadowy pines on narrow sand trails overgrown with dewberry and cotton grass. Usually we worked beside pickers who'd been bussed in from Philadelphia, but this morning it was just my brothers, the cousins, and Grandfather.

That morning, when we got to the new bog, Uncle Zach climbed from the truck and looked out over the bog, breathing deeply as we crowded just behind him.

"Is this yours?" one cousin marveled. It did, technically, butt up against Uncle Zach's western fields.

Uncle Zach smiled. "Not exactly." Then he moved away with some of the older kids to unload the picking tubs.

"I've never been here," said my eldest brother.

"Every twelve years," Grandfather said. "You were too young the last time."

"Why so long?" I asked.

"Others look after it in the meantime."

"Others?"

"Other families," he explained. Then he told us the rest.

"Fields burned the summer of thirty-four. Not the first or last time such a thing happened in the endless dry pines. Many fields had been lost in that manner, but no one had lost more than the Luker family. They were one of the first families to settle in Chatsworth, and they lost everything. More than forty acres gone in a matter of minutes. The solution seemed obvious to the remaining four farmers and their families. The four had lost much, but not quite all. When they each gave up an acre or two, some a little more, the Lukers had something to work for, to work on.

"Other families helped plant bushes and build the new dams and found extra goods to help the Lukers get by. Eleven farms in all—most of the town—had contributed something."

Grandfather had been only twenty years old when he gave his land, but as the years passed the old boundaries were eventually forgotten, lost in the greater whole. The Luker's own fields returned and the strangely shaped bog had become, as it always was, I suppose, owned again by all.

And so, Grandfather explained, "We take turns caring for it. Each year a different family—one of the twelve. Any proceeds are given to a family in need or, more often, to the entire community at the annual fall festival."

We worked hard that day, and the next, too, with new understanding and appreciation for the misshapen bog. Beating the bushes with a hose, I alone must have collected 300 pounds of berries. When the bog was harvested, we all simply sat around it and sipped our water. And stared at it. Our bog. I saw it only once more, when I was in college.

I'm thirty-six now, and you can do the math easy enough. Next year will be twenty-four years since the first time I saw the bog. Uncle Zach has passed on now, Grandfather too. But the cousins will be there. And my brother is planning to bring his daughter and son. I'll be there too.

The Elves Under the Stairs

by E. Dian Moore | *Mannington, West Virginia*

THE 1940S BIRTHED a cherished and much anticipated Christmas tradition in our family. On Thanksgiving of each year, when the family gathered in Mannington, West Virginia, each grandchild under the age of sixteen would painstakingly write a Christmas wish on a small slip of paper. One by one, we would then carefully place our wish by the crack between the fourth and fifth tread of the stairs in our grandparents' house. Breathless and jittery, we waited and watched, squealing with laughter when the wish was snatched by an elf from the other side of the crack.

As we watched, twinkling lights of red and green sometimes glimmered before a small hand at the end of a skinny, green-and-white-striped arm, appeared. Perhaps searching for another wish? Cinnamon-scented breath enchanted the child whose face was nearest the crack. Tinkling laughter tickled our young ears, while festive music played, such as we were sure was heard at the North Pole.

Occasionally, a wish was taken, only to be thrust back, startling the children into exclamations of dismay.

Our grandparents had told us the Legend of the Elves while

holding our small hands, binding us with the magic of the moment, creating a precious portrait we still carry in our hearts. Age-ripened hands, marvelously gnarled from the hard labors of love, cradled our smaller, softer hands, idle for a moment from innocent play.

What a sight it must have been. Grandparent and grandchild, tiptoeing to the stairs, their fingers and ours pressed against excited lips. And with faces resting on the tread, young and old alike watched and waited—a tender smile gracing one, the other shining with a child's wonder.

"I see one! I see one!" The same thrilled cry came, year after year, as one by one the youngsters fell headlong under the enchanted spell of the elves under the stairs.

The Legend of the Elves grew as we matured. It became a rite of passage that marked the year each of us turned sixteen—a year when enchanting secrets were revealed. First, we learned the sorrowful truth that there really weren't any tiny elves living under the stairs. Our disappointment was softened with homemade cookies and milk, and then the second and best part of the legend was revealed. Clandestine conferences were held to initiate the newly mature into the fantastic elf scheme. Not one of us said no when we were invited to be human-sized elves and take up residence under the stairs.

Each new elf was carefully trained in the art of elfmanship. Important skills had to be mastered before the newly recruited were permitted to practice elfery. We learned techniques important to the craft: silently creeping under the stairs without being seen, proper maneuvering of the elf puppets, and chewing cinnamon gum and breathing tiny elf breaths through the crack between the treads. We learned how to hit the right button on the tape player so that quiet North Pole music added to the magic. We also had to learn to plug in the twinkle lights without getting shocked, and how to giggle like an elf. Most importantly, we learned to snatch wishes like true elves!

New elves anticipated their debut with anxiety and enthusiasm.

Some of us had to mature a little more before we could handle the stress, but we all took pride in mastering the elfing skills and becoming a part of the magic of make believe.

Some elves were so accomplished at elfery that their names have lived on throughout the generations—names such as Elfrida, Melf, and Elfred. I was the amazing Delfina.

We never tired of our elf encounters and still, amid much laughter and silliness, reminisce of our adventures on both sides of the stairs.

Today, no elves live in the grand old house with steps of crack-ridden treads, but we keep the legend alive and continue to practice our skills. We elves have many a trick up our green-and-white sleeves, and are ever on the lookout for a place to once again snatch a wish. ⌒

Mama's Birthday

by Emmarie Lehnick | *Hereford, Texas*

"MAMA, IT'S YOUR BIRTHDAY," I squealed, throwing my six-year-old arms around her in a hug. "Are we going to have a special supper?"

"Of course we are," she replied. "Birthdays are important occasions in this house. We're going to have fried chicken, mashed potatoes, gravy, hot biscuits, fresh green beans, fried okra, cantaloupe, sliced tomatoes, green onions, and chocolate cake. I've got to get busy."

I didn't think it was fair that Mama had to make her own birthday cake, but she was the only one in our house who knew how to cook good stuff. Besides, every year when someone commented that she shouldn't have to bake her own cake, she replied, "It's okay. I don't mind. Each birthday is a celebration of life."

Her birthday also meant that company was coming. Uncle Mel and Aunt Alice, and Cousin Jess and Cousin Nellie were the only relatives we had in or near our little town of Hereford, Texas. Mama had also invited the newly married couple who lived across the street.

While Mama spent the morning in the kitchen, my sisters and I straightened the house, dusted, and set the big table using a starched tablecloth that had taken Mama a long time to iron.

As soon as I heard Mama's call to come lick the table knife used to spread the chocolate icing, I ran to the kitchen. With closed eyes, I let my tongue slide up one side of the knife and then down the other, until all the sweetness was gone.

After wiping the ring of chocolate from my lips, Mama sent me to the garden to pull some green onions. In the summer of 1939, our garden produced enough vegetables for canning and for sharing with all the neighbors.

When the guests started arriving, Papa came in from the garden to wash. The relatives hugged us girls and shook hands with Papa. They exclaimed over how much I had grown since they last saw me.

Mama hurried in, tying the strings of a clean bib apron around her middle, and Aunt Alice handed her a flour-sack cup towel that she had embroidered special for the occasion. Cousin Nelly brought Mama a quart of her special apple butter. After the neighbor newlyweds were introduced to everyone, the bride handed Mama a jar filled with irises from their yard. In that day and age, all birthday gifts were generally homemade, and all were appreciated. I remembered Mama telling us that homemade meant it was a gift of love because it had taken the person's time and planning to create.

Mama thanked everyone for the gifts and handed out hugs. Then she hung the cup towel over one side of the buffet so everyone could see the needlework. Using his strong grip, Cousin Jess opened the apple butter and Mama sniffed its contents then exhaled with a smile. She put a big spoon into the jar and placed it on the table. Last, she set the purple flowers in the middle of the table and stepped back to admire their beauty.

Chairs scraped the linoleum floor as we took our places at the table and held hands as Papa said the blessing. Long before the "Amen" was heard, I had my eye on the drumstick on the platter in the middle of the table.

As the heaping bowls of food were passed around the table

clockwise, I dipped the big spoon into the river of yellow butter on the mashed potatoes and decided that birthday dinners couldn't be beat.

When Mama saw that everyone had finished the main meal, she and the other ladies gathered the used plates and took them to the kitchen sink. They brought out clean saucers for everyone. "Oohs" and "aahs" voiced the approval of the three-layer chocolate birthday cake Mama proudly carried to the table.

We all joined in to sing *Happy Birthday*, and Mama began to cut the cake. Once she had passed each person a piece, Papa jumped up and asked that we wait just a minute before we dug in. He stepped onto the back porch empty-handed, but returned with a wooden ironing board with legs that folded for storage. He said he had ordered it from the Sears-Roebuck catalog.

When he handed it to Mama, her lips quivered and she wiped her eyes on the corner of her apron. Everyone at the table knew that Mama took in ironing to make extra money. The ironing board she used was a padded table leaf that rested on the back of two chairs.

Mama unfolded the wooden board, which was much shorter and narrower than the ones of today. With flushed cheeks, she invited the ladies and girls to have our cake on her new ironing board.

"After all," she said, "an ironing board is strictly for female use, and this will give the men more room to have their dessert."

I felt like I was at a ladies' tea party. We womenfolk placed our chairs around the wooden board as Mama handed us our saucers of cake. Then, like a queen, she took her place at the narrowest end of the new board. That small, wooden folding ironing board was the grandest gift I had ever seen.

Birthdays were always special at our house, but Mama's birthday that year was one of the best. I still remember the feeling of awe as we sat around the ironing board eating our dessert. But mostly, I remember the way Mama's face shone with happiness, and the look of pride in Daddy's eyes as he cradled her special present in his arms. ✎

Honest Question, Honest Answer

by David Crane Swarts | *Rushville, Indiana*

My stocky grandfather was a stern, stubborn, and shrewd farmer. We lived near him in Rushville, Indiana, and visited him often in the spacious family home that his father built in 1896. He particularly enjoyed having some or all of his seven children and their families get together for no other reason than to eat and visit. All revered and respected him; indeed, he demanded it. On those occasions when he had an audience, he would boast about how he had bested someone in a business deal, or obtained a better price for his cattle than his peers, or how he accomplished more work in less time than anyone else.

All of the adults listened dutifully, occasionally asking a leading question that required more detail. When that happened, he expanded and expounded on his success, making sure everyone understood the magnitude of his intelligence. He even tossed in a little humor once in a while. And when he smiled, you could see the small sliver of gold dental work that made the letter "T" with the stem between his two lower front teeth.

I was eight years old in 1957, and for two years I had been able to understand some of Grandpa's stories. I was just coming into my own powers of reasoning and couldn't help wondering that if it were possible for Grandpa to get the best of someone else, then it might be possible for someone else to get the better of Grandpa. And I wanted to hear *that* story.

One day, after one of these family meals, I asked my mother, "Has Grandpa ever been outsmarted?"

"Why don't you ask him," she said as she tilted her head to the side with a wry smile, which I didn't understand. It was then and there that I resolved to put the question to Grandpa the next time I saw him. And as fortune would have it, the next time I saw him was a family gathering with eight adults and ten children present. Once again, as if on cue, Grandpa started to relate one of his success stories and everyone was listening politely. When he had finished, I piped up.

"Grandpa?"

"Yes, David?"

"Have you ever been outsmarted?" I asked, respectfully.

The minute my question was out of my mouth, the floodgates of laughter opened and all the adults guffawed uncontrollably, with Grandma's laughter being the loudest. All, that is, except Grandpa. And just as suddenly as the laughter erupted, the room went dead silent. Everyone looked at Grandpa, waiting for his answer.

He put his hand to his chin and looked out the window for what seemed to be an eternity. I could see the wheels turning in his head and I can now surmise what his thoughts probably were: *Darn good question. The boy has no hidden agenda, no ulterior motive. Been shootin' my mouth off again. Braggin'. Shouldn't do that. Now what do I say? David deserves a darn good answer to a darn good question. Aha! I've got it!*

His eyes brightened, he looked at me with his big wide grin, and I swear I saw that gold "T" sparkle in the sunlight. He leaned close to me, still smiling, and wagged his stubby finger.

"Never by the same feller twice!" he replied smartly.

Laughter erupted again. This time, Grandpa was laughing too. It was an honest answer and sage advice. Grandpa retained his dignity, and I have never forgotten. ✍

Sisters on Vacation

by Anna M. Popescu | *Largo, Florida*

I WAS EXHAUSTED AFTER BEING ON AN AIRPLANE ALL DAY, but my fatigue was tempered by excitement at seeing my sisters again. I disembarked and lugged my suitcase toward the main terminal for what seemed like miles. As I rounded a curve in the walkway, someone shouted my name. I looked up and saw my sisters standing a few feet away. I broke into a huge smile when I saw the sign they held above their heads: my name printed in huge letters, just like a chauffeur would have.

In the next instant, I was enveloped in hugs, all of us trying to talk at once.

My four sisters and I live in various parts of the country. Two live in the Northeast, another two are in Florida, and I live in northern Arizona, all the way across the country. This scattering of family makes it difficult for all of us to get together in one place, but our annual Sisters' Vacation is something we cherish, and none of us would miss it.

I'm the oldest, and though fifteen years separates my youngest sister and me, the age difference is barely noticeable now that we're all adults. In spite of the age spread and the various places we live, the similarities among us are striking. We all have some degree of the curly dark hair that denotes our Italian heritage, and we each have two children. No matter where we go, people do a double-take because we all look so much alike.

A couple of years ago, we decided to meet in Orlando, Florida, to do some shopping and tour Universal Studios, and then travel to Largo to reunite with our parents. We hadn't seen each other in more than a year and were really excited to have this special time together. We got very little sleep that first night as we shared snacks and caught up with the events in each other's lives. We're fairly good about keeping in touch by e-mail, but some things just can't be conveyed through cyberspace.

We couldn't wait to get to Universal Studios that first day. Even threatening rain clouds didn't dampen our enthusiasm. We were happy just to be together. The nasty weather held off for the first hour, but then the clouds opened up and we were caught in a downpour. We were immediately drenched and didn't waste any time joining the long line to purchase rain ponchos.

What a sight we were in our powder-blue ponchos stamped with the Universal Studios insignia. It took some time for our clothes to dry under the ponchos, but we kept touring the park anyway. A little rain wouldn't ruin our day, and the photos we now share prove it: five women with dark, damp, frizzy hair lined up in light-blue ponchos and huge smiles.

When my sisters and I get together, we have the time of our lives. People give us amused glances as they pass by because we're usually laughing about something one of us has said or seen. That's when we turn to them in unabashed chorus and proclaim loudly, "We're sisters, and we're on vacation!"

Even though we're a close-knit family, life sometimes gets in the way, making it difficult for us to always agree or be completely comfortable with one another. Differences of opinion, distance, and unresolved disputes have conspired to place a wedge in the constancy of our affection for each other. But when all is said and done, we are five women with a common, very tight-knit bond: We are sisters.

We've learned that it doesn't matter how unique or disparate our opinions. It makes no difference that we don't all think alike. In fact, our differences are what make us a strong family unit.

On our last vacation, I was the first one to leave. At the airport, my sisters waited with me as I checked in. We shared one last hug, and then I joined the long line to the security checkpoint. About ten minutes later, as I was inching forward in this seemingly endless line, I once again heard my name being shouted. I looked to the left, and there were all four of my sisters—waving, laughing, and shouting my name. I waved back and threw them a kiss. Several people behind me smiled at our unbridled enthusiasm.

"We're sisters," I informed them, nodding at the four women who were still waving at me. "And we were on vacation!" ❧

As the Wedding March Played

by Garnet Hunt White | *Doniphan, Missouri*

MY STORY BEGINS SOME YEARS AGO, when Glenn White and I were traveling in a car down a creek bed road in the lowlands. As water gurgled around our tires, Glenn slowed the car and reached into his pocket. His hand brought out a small box, and he opened it. A diamond ring and a wedding band sparkled in the sunlight. With water splashing against the fenders, he reached for my left hand and said, "Garnet, I love . . ."

Wham!

The impact of the car slamming into something knocked us against our seat belts.

"What . . . what happened?" we gasped as the front of the car shot upward and the back end and trunk sank downward.

Glenn had been concentrating on me and not on his driving, and rocks in the creek had turned the car wheels. Now the front end was on the creek bank and the back end was in three feet of water. When the car lurched sideways, the jewelry box fell to the floorboards. Glenn quickly grabbed it. With shaking hands, he put the diamond on the third finger of my left hand.

"Set a date," he whispered with hoarse authority. "I'll be there." Then he jumped from the car and into the water.

The romantic moment vanished as Glenn pushed the car, and I guided it in neutral. After what seemed an eternity, Glenn managed to heave and shove the car off the rocks.

I will never forget that day—November 20, 1955. I rode in the car that day with soggy, cold Glenn, my left hand wearing his diamond engagement ring and holding his wet arm. Stunned, we didn't talk until we got to my parents' home and Glenn changed into dry clothes.

A week later, we decided January 15, 1956, would be an excellent date to get married. We even discussed where we would live, but in the back of my mind I kept thinking that Glenn hadn't really proposed to me.

On our wedding day, our kinfolks and friends filled the church. I stood in my white, flowing wedding gown in the church parlor and peeked out. I saw Grandpa McKinney, Uncle Guy, and Aunt Essie sitting in the first row, with space left for Mother and Papa to sit, later. The next rows held cousins. Friends filled the pews to the back of the church.

Pressing my nose into the door crack, I saw Glenn's parents and his relatives on the right hand side of the church.

"What's Pastor Edward eying?" I whispered to myself. My mouth formed the word "Oh" as I spotted the object of his concern. The big white bow attached to the pew that held Glenn's parents dangled. On closer inspection, I realized Glenn's father was fidgeting with it. Was he nervous about gaining a daughter-in-law? Glancing down the aisle, I noticed that all the other bows rested quietly, like the people as they waited for Glenn and me to become man and wife.

Suddenly I heard my college roommate, Ruth, begin to play the wedding march. I snatched up my wedding gown train and stood there. Fear, stark and vivid, knotted inside of me.

"I've got to see Glenn," I declared.

Mother and Papa, who together would give me away, and the others in the wedding party all spoke at once. "You're not supposed to see each other until you walk into the church."

"I must." My voice quivered as I started for the door. "I've got to see Glenn."

"You're not stopping the wedding, are you?" someone asked.

I didn't answer. I just stood there, unsure of everything except my need to speak to Glenn.

"All right," Papa said. "I'll get Glenn."

"And I want to see him alone," I cried, tears welling up in my eyes.

Papa brought Glenn to the room and left us alone. My groom-to-be took me in his arms, kissed my tears away, and asked, "Darling, what's wrong?"

"Glenn, you never asked me to marry you!"

"Is that it?" Glenn laughed. "I can do something about that."

The notes of the wedding march sounded as Glenn tenderly sat me in a chair. The sound quickly faded into the background. To me, my lover's proposal was the only thing I wanted to hear. Later, my kin and friends would laugh at this last-minute ritual between Glenn and me, and Grandpa McKinney would ask what had been so important that we couldn't wait until we were married, adding that he had been in a hurry for a piece of wedding cake. But it wouldn't matter to me. All I had eyes for at that moment was Glenn. He knelt before me and took my hand in his. With impressive sincerity, he said, "Garnet, my precious gem. I couldn't go on living without you. Darling, will you marry me within the next fifteen minutes?"

I kissed him, my fears melting. Then I looked at him and whispered, "I will." ❧

A Pear in the Sand

by Candy Killion | *Verona, New Jersey*

It was the turn of the nineteenth century. A young doctor wiped sweat from his brow, smiling broadly as the big stone wheel turned. The dam he had built a year ago still held, and now the gristmill was turning. Just what this town needed, Dr. Christopher Bone thought, and worth the extra work. His homestead, high in the Watchung Mountains, was filled with verdant valleys and good hardwood. He dipped a tin cup into the Peckman River and drank. It was a good place, this Verona.

The dam held fast that day and many others, and by the time the son of his son had been buried nearby and the old wheel had stopped turning, a lake had been born. Verona Lake was named for the sleepy, happy town its waters kissed.

By the late 1920s, the miller's homestead had become a park, and a century of children had dipped their feet in the lake's steady, calm waters and spread blankets on the grass for picnic lunches.

During one such picnic, a small boy with bear-brown eyes and tousled black curls clung to his father's hand, and his mother trailed behind them. Clad in a crisp white shirt and knickers, the boy spied his favorite pear tree and was delighted that no one else had claimed the spot. He slipped from his father's grip, running and unbuttoning his shoes at the same time.

"Daddy, Daddy! There, c'mon!"

"On with you!" The older man laughed, watching his son lose his footing on a discarded shoe and roll end over end under the shade of the pear tree.

"I suppose this is it, hmm?" the woman asked. Receiving no answer, she turned to her husband, but he and the boy were already gone to the riverbank, long pants and knickers rolled up as far as they could, splashing the Reilly kids from down the street as they waded in. She spread her old tablecloth on the thick grass and leaned against the comfortable, familiar trunk. The breeze coming off the lake tickled her bare toes. She closed her eyes. It was a good day for a nice, quiet Fourth of July birthday.

"Up with you, Gal," a voice called. "You know you ought to be dancin' today!"

The woman's eyes flew open as a handful of fresh lilacs were tossed into her lap, startling her, just for a moment. They were here— nearly all of them. Her big brother John, bringing flowers like always. And Kitty and Betty and Frank and Margaret, who was holding another of her awful spice cakes and sporting a big freckled grin. And there, just over the hill, waving to her, were more family members.

Smiling broadly, the woman broke into a jig, kicking her heels and flapping her skirts.

"Do you think Mama was surprised?" the boy asked, racing his father to the riverbank.

"Hardly," his father answered with a knowing grin. It wasn't the surprise that mattered; it was the gathering.

Laughing, he and his son joined the rest of the clan spreading tablecloths in the shade. By the time darkness fell, all the neighbors had arrived as well: the Scotts and the Reds and the Corts. Many of them had stayed on longer at the parade, but there was room for everyone there by the lakeside. The boy was tired now. He yawned a little and curled up near his mother.

"Better stay up, boy!" His father chuckled, and tickled him under the arm just to be sure. Leaves rustled, and a pear fell from above onto the child's head. The boy was wide-awake now, and they all laughed.

The first "*Kaboom*!!" lit up the sky over the lake, the fizz and blast of Roman candles filling the July night. The boy scrunched up his nose, taking in the aroma of lake air, Independence Day smoke, and the faint scent of pears. He decided not to eat the fruit that had fallen from the tree. He wanted to remember tonight forever.

Before they left with their neighbors, the boy scooped up some sand from the bank and filled one of his mother's empty Mason jars with it, the one that had held pickled eggs. He picked up some of the dirty spatterware plates from the picnic, too, so it looked like he was helping. Back home, in his darkened bedroom, he carefully laid the pear in butcher paper and poured the sand over it, tying the whole package with twine and setting it in the back of his closet. And then he forgot about it, as he played kick-the-can and hide-and-seek in Verona Park.

The package in the closet sat intact and forgotten. It was moved absentmindedly with his skates and baseball bat when the time had come to leave Verona, his lovely Verona, for the city. His grandfather had died, and his grandmother was alone now in her big city house. The boy stood one last time under his pear tree and looked out over the lake.

❦

The boy had grown and become a man with bear-brown eyes. His curls gone now, lost in a heap at his feet at Fort Dix. They would grow back when this was all over. Now he sat on a mountain in Italy, artillery fire in the distance, a far cry from the swoosh and flash of Roman candles. His feet had not been bare for a long time. Rather, they were swaddled in several pairs of coarse wool GI socks, protection against the assault of a Po Valley winter.

It was cold, and he was afraid.

Mail call interrupted his thoughts and he anxiously reached for the bundle tossed his way. Ma had come through, as always. He ripped open her letter with the enthusiasm of a kid in knickers, and read: "I found this, Robert. I think you might need it."

He scratched under his helmet, behind his ear, and wondered. Homemade cookies? Some more writing paper? Another book? Whatever it was, it would be fine. Ma always seemed to know what to send.

He tore into the parcel and carefully unwrapped the twine and butcher paper. Within, he found a pear, perfectly preserved, the afterthought of an eight-year-old so many summers ago. The sand had done its petrifying work. There was another note inside in his mother's handwriting, a simple message that meant so much: "The lake. I remember."

And a world away, the boy with the tousled curls sat on a hill, breathing in the smell of fresh green grass and the lake where the gristmill used to be. His rifle was by his side, but he was home, in Verona.&

The Township of
Verona, New Jersey

Population: 13,500

Town Facts

First incorporated • Verona was established in the mid-nineteenth century and was officially incorporated in 1907. Verona got its name by compromise. The first choice, Vernon, was already taken.

Former names • Before the Revolutionary War, Verona was part of a 14,000-acre tract purchased from the Lenape Indians, originally designated as the Horse Neck section of Newark. The area celebrated its independence from Newark after the war and merged with the Township of Caldwell, carrying that name until the mid-1800s.

Location • Verona is nestled among the Watchung Mountains (specifically between the first and second mountains), in northeastern New Jersey, near East Orange and just eight miles from Newark, the state's industrial, commercial hub. New York City is 24 miles northeast of Verona.

Industry • Primarily residential, with light industry and retail commerce, Verona is a modern, bustling community with an intimate small-town feel.

The Unbehauens of Verona

Bob Unbehauen, contributor Candy Killion's father, is "the boy" in "A Pear in the Sand."

Though he was born in bustling Newark, his parents settled in sleepy, tranquil Verona shortly thereafter. From 1922 until the early '30s, he climbed Verona's trees and played ball on its quiet, friendly streets. Later, though he had grown and moved away, he took his daughter back to beloved Verona Park many, many times. It was there, at lakeside as a child, that she lay daydreaming on the park's lush grass, watching white clouds in a brilliant blue sky change shapes and begin to whisper their stories.

Fate took Bob many places after the first decade of his life spent in Verona's embrace, but Verona remained—to the end—his hometown of heart.

Interesting Facts

Verona's school system has been lauded as one of *Money* magazine's "100 Best Buys" in housing and education in the United States. Additionally, Verona is truly a kid-friendly place. Annually, the township sponsors "International Walk to School Day" to help promote children's physical fitness, environmental awareness, and sense of community. .

Interesting People

Verona is the hometown of comedian/actor Jay Mohr (*Last Comic Standing, Mad TV, CSI Miami,* and *The West Wing*), and actress Robyn Petty, who appeared in the film *Midnight Madness.* During World War I, Verona's first battle casualty was Sgt. Frank Wittenweiler; he was also the first of Verona's military members to receive the Purple Heart.

Places of Note

Verona Park is the township's crown jewel. Fifty-four acres of flowerbeds, lawns, and trees surround placid thirteen-acre Verona Lake. In the 1800s, the beautiful scenery brought nature lovers by horse, foot, and eventually by trolley to swim and picnic on the banks.

Today, Verona Park boasts a playground, softball and tennis courts, a concert area, and a fitness path. The Wallenberg Bridge, which runs through the park, is named in memory of humanitarian Raoul Wallenberg, a Swedish businessman believed to be responsible for saving the lives of 100,000 Hungarian Jews from Hitler's "final solution."

Grandmother's Imagination

by Patricia Wilson | *Lancaster, New Hampshire*

WHEN I WAS A CHILD, my grandmother, Persis Beach Bennett, delighted me with the music she wrote. She wrote Christian songs, children's songs, and love songs. This was especially fascinating to me because Grammie was blind. One summer day in 1949, when I was eight years old, Grammie sat on the piano bench, placed one finger on the piano keys, and taught me a special song she'd written just for me. I knew then that although my grandmother couldn't see, she could imagine.

Grammie wanted to preserve the music she'd written, but because she was blind, she wasn't able to physically put the words and notes to paper. Her only hope for saving the music for her family was to record it. With her daughter Beulah at the piano, she recorded fifteen of her songs on old seventy-eight vinyl albums.

Her plan worked. The whole family loved the music and played the records often. Grammie's music became an important part of family get-togethers. With time and wear, the records fell into ruin, having been played over and over again. By the time my generation entered the picture, the records had so badly deteriorated the music was impossible to hear. The music that brought joy and love to so many family events was going to be lost forever if somebody didn't do something to preserve it.

In July of 1994, I visited my cousins in New England. Beulah's son and I searched her old home in Vermont for our grandmother's written music, but the search turned up nothing. But another cousin found Grammie's records in her New Hampshire basement. I took the records with me when I returned to Oregon and decided I would try to decipher them at my own home. As I carried them in my lap on the plane trip home, the enormity of the project hit me. How on earth did I think I could accomplish this task?

Ignoring my blooming reservations, I began my mission to save Grammie's music. To avoid adding more scratches to the records, I made a tape of each of the songs. For an entire year, I tried to decipher the lyrics. The task was proving to be impossible, and I was losing hope. Then, one day I received a surprise call from Beulah's son in Vermont.

"Pat!" he exclaimed. "You're going to flip. I found the written music."

I remembered back when I was seventeen, in 1958, when I had tried to work with Beulah to get some of Grammie's music written down. We managed to finish only three songs, and I had been worried that even though Beulah was a delightful woman, she was too high-strung and nervous to ever complete the project on her own. I was sure that the music would be lost forever.

I was wrong. Beulah passed away several years ago, but to my surprise, she spent the thirty years before her death writing down as much of Grammie's work as she could. Ninety percent of it was in the packet her son sent me.

In the beginning, I wasn't trying to do anything grand. My goal was simply to try to save the music for my family. It took ten years, but with God's help and the help of many talented people in central Oregon, all fifteen of Grammie's songs have been reproduced. A CD titled *Songs from Grandmother's House* now holds all of her music and includes a picture of her and her lifelong home in New Hampshire.

I was so pleased with the end product that I decided to write a children's book about my grandmother and her music, using five of her children's songs.

Because it's so generic, the book could be about any grandmother and any grandchildren in any town. But people in Lancaster, New Hampshire, know it is their town. My grandmother would be delighted to know that, today, hundreds of children are enjoying her songs as much as I did when I was a child.

When I think back to 1949, when Grammie was teaching me my song, "Patty's Puppy Pepper," I never dreamed I would be the one to preserve our family's history as well as help children everywhere learn to overcome their disabilities by developing other talents. But Grammie taught my whole family that we could imagine.∽

The Memory Boxes

by Kristine Ziemnik | *Chippewa Lake, Ohio*

THANKSGIVING AT OUR HOUSE is filled with family traditions and it is always a joyous occasion. Immediately following grace, each member of the family tells what he or she personally has to be thankful for. After dinner, we all drift to the living room to catch up on family news.

One Thanksgiving, while everyone was relaxing, I ducked down to the basement to bring up my son David's memory boxes. It wasn't until the end of the evening that I would realize my basement is indeed something to be most thankful for.

When my children were born, I wanted to save items from their childhood days for later retrieval, so I made all four of them what I called a "memory box." Their memory boxes are just cardboard boxes from the grocery store with nice lids—but the contents are more precious than gold.

The memory boxes hold such things as newspaper clippings, greeting cards, and christening candles. When kindergarten came along, I explained to each child that they couldn't save every picture or school project, but they could choose the most special ones to add to their memory boxes.

My intention was that when my children were grown and ready to leave home, they could take their childhood memories and mementoes with them. But when our eldest son, Brian, moved to Chicago, he sorted through his memory box and threw most of the mementoes into the trash. I was heartbroken. After he left, I went through the discarded pile and packed the majority of the items back into his memory box and then stored the box in the basement. *Brian lives in a small apartment,* I reasoned. *He might appreciate his second-grade artwork at a later date.*

Before our eldest daughter, Andrea, married, she also went through her memory box, lightening the load tremendously. Was it any wonder that I picked through her wastebasket the next day and rescued some old report cards and a few Garbage Pail Kids collector cards? Andrea's things were put back into the basement next to Brian's.

And so, I decided it was time for our married son, David, to go through his memory box. Since the family was together for the holidays, I thought it would be a good opportunity to relive his fondest childhood memories with him. His wife, Lisa, enjoyed reading his report cards, and cringed appropriately as he reread his old love letters. With pumpkin pie and ice cream in hand, we critiqued his artwork and laughed uproariously as he reread "books" he had written in grade school. In college, David had been a reporter for a local newspaper, so we were duly impressed by his fourth-grade wish to be a journalist.

I bit my tongue as David dropped pieces of his past into the trash receptacle, but the whole family chuckled as he rechecked old birthday cards before discarding them, just in case some money had inadvertently been missed. When he pulled the snip of hair from his first haircut out of the box, memories and emotions flooded my mind.

"If you are going to throw that away, I wish you would do it at home," I said.

I could not watch him discard this lock of hair, something so precious to me, so I left the room. To keep my mind occupied, I busied myself in the kitchen preparing take-home packets of pie and goodies for family members who would soon be returning to their own homes. That night, I went to bed emotionally and physically exhausted.

I surmised that the reason I was so upset about the way my children pitched their memories was because they were my memories as well. My husband and I had spent so much time coaching David, helping him reach his dream of becoming a journalist, that I felt partly responsible for the A-plus he received in fifth grade for a book called *The Duck Who Wouldn't Quack*. We had gone to every one of our son's soccer games, regardless of inclement weather. The scads of paper were more than just soccer game programs. They were the records of our lives.

Was I being too sentimental?

That night, after the guests left, I lay in bed wide awake, thinking. Unable to sleep, I flipped the blanket back and got out of bed. When our children had children of their own, I could only hope they would keep the memory-box tradition alive. Turning the corner into the kitchen, my mind wandered to our youngest child, Beth. In the not-too-distant future, I would be handing Beth her cherished memory box and be forced to go through this painful ritual again. As I snapped on the kitchen light, I decided to save myself future trauma; I would ask her to go through the box alone in her apartment.

Pleased with my decision, I quickly moved toward the trash—brimming with David's memory collection—and the task at hand. Several minutes later, my bare feet touched the cold basement steps and a small smile touched my lips. I was suddenly very thankful for my large basement.❧

A Sure Thing

by LB Brumage | *Mannington, West Virginia*

WE LIVED AMONG THE HILLS AND VALLEYS of West Virginia during the Great Depression. Our little community was already so poor that the Depression didn't hit us hard like it did other folks. My father couldn't always find work, so my mother took in other people's wash to help keep food on the table. We usually had plenty to eat, even though it was mostly pinto beans and potatoes. It embarrasses me to think of how we complained at having to eat the same thing morning, noon, and night. But I guess that's just what kids do because they don't know any better.

The summer days of my youth seemed to go on forever. My sisters and I roamed the hills, wild and carefree like the squirrels that played in the hickory tree behind our house. We stayed out until dark and then, grudgingly, came home exhausted and smelling like the earth.

During the winter months, we all got a little restless from being cooped up in the house, so it was a real treat for us when our cousins stayed overnight. We slept six or eight to a bed—although I'm not sure we got much sleep. We wiggled and giggled and carried on long into the night. When we got too loud, my mother would yank open the door and yell, "Quiet!" We'd all jump and squeal like little pigs. And heaven help us if one of the little ones got scared and wet themselves, we'd all scatter like field mice and the whole house would be in an uproar until Mom could get us settled back into bed.

Some of my favorite childhood memories are of sneaking out to watch the grownups play cards after the other children had fallen asleep. From the outside looking in, card playing seemed almost magical. It was a place where adults behaved more like kids than grownups. All the worries that followed them through the day seemed to evaporate at night when the card table came out. The longer they played, the more they laughed. I'd never seen adults act so childish. For the longest time, I thought I'd stumbled onto a secret grown-up ritual, and somehow that made me feel special.

When I was finally old enough to stay up late, I was allowed to watch the game as long as I didn't ask too many questions. Those were my first uncertain steps on the road to adulthood.

Sometimes the men played poker, but usually everyone played a game called Cinch. Some folks know it as Set-Back, although not too many people outside West Virginia have ever heard of it. It plays a little bit like Pinochle, but you use regular cards or what we call a "straight deck." I've played all kinds of games in my life, but if you ask me, there's just nothing like Cinch. It's been much more than a game to me. It's been a constant companion, a friend, and a teacher. It's where I learned some of life's most important lessons like, "You've got to play the hand you're dealt" and "Everything can turn on one bad choice."

Playing Cinch is one of the traditions that held my family together as we suffered losses and celebrated good fortune. It's where my uncles offered up sage advice: "You've gotta get in there and play! Nobody ever won by watching other men play the game." That same advice sent their sons to war, and it was over cards that we silently prayed for their safe return. I learned as much about friendship and courage at a card table as anywhere else in my life. It's where I discovered the pleasure of companionship, the value of family, and the gift of laughter.

Our stories have all been passed down from generation to generation over a deck of cards. Playing cards helps challenge young minds and keeps the old ones limber. We planned marriages, healed wounds, raised kids, and watched as the world went crazy, all while playing Cinch. It was during those late-night gatherings that I began to realize all things are possible, and forgiveness, if you let it, will come as easy as the next hand.

The world has become a much different place today than it was when we were young. Nowadays, my kids have kids of their own. To my great delight, our oldest granddaughter has embraced card playing and I'm guessing it won't be long until the youngest is ready to claim her place at the table, too.

Of course, I don't get to see my family as much as I'd like. Everything just keeps moving faster and faster. But when they do come to visit, one thing is almost certain: cards at the kitchen table. It's where we come to laugh and tell stories and make new memories to mix in with the old.

Cards have helped define our family—they are part of the glue that holds us together and the Silly Putty that makes the ride so much more fun. I can only hope that future generations make time for the simple pleasures of family and friendship, no matter how far the world spins ahead.

As for me, there will always be Cinch. ✑

Threshing Adventures on the Farm

by Lucinda Rickett Strine | *Nova, Ohio*

WHO CAN FORGET the intensely hot and hard work of threshing wheat and oats in mid-summer? How excited our family was when it was our turn, and the huge steel separator chugged up the road to our farm the night before the work was to begin!

After its majestic arrival in the barnyard on our homestead southeast of Nova, Ohio, we were allowed to touch and look closely at its innards. The next day would be the high point of the summer for the young lads of the family, who would get to watch and help while this threshing machine separated the wheat and oats from the chaff and threw out the straw in a big pile.

I remember the point in my childhood when we made the switch from horses to tractors to pull the binder. The tractor that provided the power to run the thresher was a very dangerous steam engine. This engine was connected to the thresher by a long belt and pulley. Youngsters had to stay far away when this apparatus was in operation. During my teen years, we used smaller, safer tractors with gasoline engines.

Back then, as it remains today, the job was a family affair. Family and neighbors from around the southeast area of rural Nova, Ohio, drove up with their wagons. With a driver and two helpers, one to load from the ground and one to place each sheaf on the wagon, they hurriedly loaded the wagon. Then they rushed to the thresher to unload into its wide mouth. The noise was fierce as it chewed the grain loose from the straw. The hot sweaty men could pause only now and again to mop their sweating brows with red bandanas.

During this time, the womenfolk would rustle up a meal to be remembered all winter long. Each housewife tried to outdo the next in providing the best food and desserts.

To make sure everything was ready in time, the youngest child was posted to watch for the arrival of the crew from the barnyard. A couple basins of cold water, with towels and soap nearby, were put out on an old chair under a shade tree at the back of the house. Here the threshers washed off the chaff and perspiration. A barrel of clean cistern water was also set out, to refill the basins.

We often had ten to fifteen hungry men to feed. We girls helped Mom serve and waited quietly in the background until the workers were finished. We silently hoped they would not eat all the luscious pies—usually blackberry or elderberry—that Mom had baked the day before.

One of our neighbors, originally from Hungary, always pleased Mom greatly with his Old World manners as he proclaimed graciously, "Thanks for the delicious meal and the making of it." Mom blushed prettily at this.

After the workers left, we cleared the table and sat down to enjoy a more leisurely meal. The menu was always hearty: roast beef with plenty of rich brown gravy over fluffy, buttered potatoes, green beans from the garden, coleslaw from homegrown cabbage, sliced tomatoes, and perhaps chocolate cake. Seconds were almost mandatory. But it was the fruit pies everyone waited for most of all.

Wheat harvest was usually the last of July with the oats ripening about two weeks later. Harvesting oats was just as exciting as wheat threshing. On top of all the usual thrills were the shrill calls of the locusts in the trees.

Our family often cooled off after a strenuous day of threshing by sitting on the front porch, eating chilled curds and whey, and listening to the chorus of chirping crickets, buzzing cicadas, and the clear tones of katydids in the cool of the eventide breezes. How peaceful it was.

Here in Amishland, where I live today, we have the delightful vicarious memories of observing this event of fifty or sixty years ago without all the intense effort and heavy workload. The Plain People determine the order of who threshes first by lot. The last farmer in the draw may have much rain damage before it is his turn.

The farmers cut the grain with a horse-pulled binder, which also ties twine around each small bundle, called a sheaf. Then, sturdy workers, often including the women of the household, stand nine sheaves up, three on the two sides, one on each end, and one on top like an umbrella, to form a tent-like structure. This shock of grain is designed to allow rain to run off easily.

In my small village of Mt. Eaton, I find it very comforting to be surrounded by Amish farmers who re-enact daily the farming customs of my early years. I salute the industrious farmers of yesteryear, and those of my heritage, as well as all rural workers of the soil, who know firsthand what is necessary in order to gather the bounty of the farming seasons.

My hope for them is that they make time, on occasion, to relax and perhaps listen to the chorus of the insects singing to their mates at twilight time, at the end of a scorching summer day, as I do still.

Grandma's Roses

by David L. Barber | *Mathis, Texas*

GRANDMA LOVED ROSES. Her entire yard was covered with every kind and size imaginable, the soft perfume a treat to those passing by her south Texas home. She cared for each one like it was a small child, cupping her hands around the blossoms and cuddling up to them, talking to them. She always commented on how delightful it would be for all of them to be in bloom at once. But with eight children, she didn't have time to dwell on wishful thinking, as there was always something that needed her attention. The house needed to be cleaned, Paul needed help with this, Leonard with that. It took many hours to tend a large family and much love. She had plenty, not just for her family but for others in need as well.

"God will provide what we need," she would say sincerely.

My grandparents weren't well off by any means. Grandma depended on God to take care of her, and she shared, in her quiet and gentle way, whatever she got with others. This New Orleans–bred lady never turned anyone down. When the homeless passed through during the rough times, she was there to feed them, provide clothing, and care for them in much the same way she tended her roses.

◄❖►

She was known throughout the community for her roses and for her kindness.

After we were all grown, Grandma had more time for her garden. We'd drive out to visit and see her in her apron, toiling among the buds and blooms. She'd smile and say, "One day, all of my roses will bloom at the same time!" Then she'd shoo us inside and fix plates of sweet cakes for everyone, hurrying around the table until we were all taken care of. She was never caught off guard.

But time has a way of catching up with you, and one year Grandma slowed down. Her stride wasn't as fast. She sat in the garden to tend her roses now. When she took sick, the roses showed the illness too. They hung their canes and looked sad as the weeks went on and on. The family had to fend for themselves, and it was a difficult adjustment. There were plenty of hands, but it just wasn't the same. The years had taken their toll.

We sadly made the long trip to Mathis on a sunny, spring day, and cried that morning as they laid Grandma to rest. Afterward, we returned to the house to visit with family. As we pulled into the gravel driveway, we burst into a fresh stream of tears. All of Grandma's roses were in glorious bloom.

The Screen House

by Alice A. Mendelsohn | *Carbondale, Pennsylvania*

IN THE DAYS FOLLOWING THE GREAT DEPRESSION, families struggled. Money was tight in every household. Folks couldn't afford to go out on the town, so families and neighbors got together and made their own fun, at very little cost to any one family in particular.

In our little coal-mining town, the mention of a party was always welcome information, especially if Hazel's name was attached to it.

Hazel could form a party at the drop of a hat. She miraculously found food, every time. Even without notice, the table would be overflowing. If Hazel mentioned a party, it was as if a signal went through town announcing fun times on Canaan Street. Weather didn't matter. Rain or shine, people gathered in Hazel's yard.

One summer day, about an hour into a party celebrating my Aunt Marie's birthday, the skies opened up and everyone ran for cover. With so many people in the backyard, there was only so much protection beneath the fruit trees and under the grape arbors. Unable to take shelter, most of the family grabbed up belongings and headed home, ending the festivities.

As Hazel cleared up the rain-soaked food, plates, and implements, she wondered aloud, "Wouldn't it be nice to have a screened-in picnic area for a day such as this?" Almost before the words were uttered, she recalled an ad in the local paper featuring screened tents for $100. It was as if a light bulb above her head turned on with a click. The only question was: Where could she get that kind of money?

People in town were slowly recovering from the Depression. There was no work, barely enough money to put food on the table or clothes on their backs. How could she even dream of gathering $100 for a screen house? But she wasn't one to quit an idea once she had one, and before long she came up with a plan. She would hold a raffle.

She immediately put her plan into action. First she stopped at Uncle Jimmy's print shop and placed an order for 200 raffle tickets. If she could sell 200 tickets at $1 each, she could raffle off one screen house and keep the other for her own family gatherings.

Everyone in our small town knew, loved, and trusted Hazel—most of the population was related to her in some way. Selling the tickets was a snap. Everyone pitched in and helped sell tickets to friends and neighbors. Before long, all of the raffle books were sold. Hazel immediately walked into Blum's store with the money, and walked out with two screen houses.

All ticket holders were invited to her house the following Wednesday for a two o'clock drawing. One of the tents was assembled. The other was left in the box.

The circle of expectant winners widened as two o'clock drew near. Not to be accused of unfairness, one of the local children was asked to pick the winning ticket. Tommy stuck his arm way down into the bucket, withdrew one pink ticket, and grinned as he handed it to Hazel. With no further hesitation or fanfare, she called out the number "2-5-5-2."

From deep within the circle a woman screamed, "It's me! It's me!" She ran up to the sealed crate containing the unopened screen house and shouted again happily, "It's mine! It's mine!"

Everyone agreed this had been another successful party at Hazel's: success for the elated winner and also for Hazel, who was now the proud owner of a long-dreamed-of screened-in picnic area. The screen house made it possible for the entire family and community to gather for parties and reunions at any time of the day or night, regardless of inclement weather. And though Hazel was too modest to accept credit for the parties that were held from that day forward, we all knew without her ingenuity there never would have been a raffle, nor a screen house that was open to all.

The Uninvited Visitor

by Renie Burghardt | *Doniphan, Missouri*

THE SMALL OZARK TOWN OF DONIPHAN, MISSOURI, is nestled in the beautiful Current River Valley. Sprinkled within and around its borders are numerous quaint little country churches, where families, large and small, gather together for Sunday worship services.

A couple of years ago, in late summer, I attended one of these Sunday services with a friend. Tall, spreading oaks surrounded this particular small, white church. The windows and doors of the church had been opened to allow the cool morning breeze to enter, and to my delight, we sat in the third pew on the left, near one of the open windows.

A small congregation of about forty people settled down and soon joined forces in praising the Lord with a hymn. Directly in front of me sat a family of four: mother, father, grandmother, and a young boy, who was five or six years old. He had hair the color of straw, and the voice of an angel, for he sang along quite loudly and sweetly, knowing all the words of the hymn.

The minister walked up to the pulpit to give the sermon. "Today," he began, but was quickly interrupted by a cheerful and loud sound that rang throughout the little church.

Chirp! Chirp! Chirp!

"Well, it seems we have an uninvited visitor among us, this morning," the minister said, bemused but somewhat annoyed at the interruption.

Chirp! Chirp!

The sound rang out again and a murmur rose as the congregation glanced around, searching for the culprit. The little boy quickly turned to his left, then to his right. He looked directly behind him and then glanced up at us, his face intense. I couldn't help but smile.

"As I was saying . . ." the minister began again.

Chirp! Chirp! Chirp! The uninvited visitor continued singing loudly.

Soon, everyone was looking to our side of the church. The uninvited visitor was somewhere in our vicinity. People glanced under the pews, feet poised to eradicate the noisy little bug.

Chirp! Chirp!

"There he is," whispered an elderly man directly in front of the boy, his foot thrusting forward. But just before his shoe could come down on the black chirper, the little boy dove under the pew.

"Brian! What are you doing?" his father whispered loudly.

Despite his father's reprimanding tone and his mother's attempt to pull him back up, the boy wriggled forward and captured the noisy critter.

During the commotion, the grandma, apparently aware of the workings of the young boy, smiled tolerantly.

"I got him!" Brian announced loudly, as he emerged with tightly cupped hands. "He's just doin' what crickets do. I'll take him on outside and let him go. He shouldn't be squashed just for doin' what crickets do."

The young boy hurried down the aisle toward the back door, keeping his hands tightly cupped. As he reached the exit, someone opened the door for him and he disappeared.

By this time, everyone in the congregation was smiling and nodding. The minister waited until the boy came back inside and rejoined his family in the pew. Then, with one last smile directed at the lad, he returned to the service.

With a sparkle in her eye, the boy's grandma leaned down and tousled his hair affectionately. "You've made the Lord smile this morning with your good deed, Brian."

While the uninvited visitor chirped gaily outside the small country church where families worshiped together, the boy with the straw-colored hair—obviously proud of his good deed—joined in the singing even more enthusiastically than before.⟳

THE TOWN OF

Doniphan, Missouri

Population: 1,932

Town Facts

First incorporated • Doniphan, named after Missouri's Mexican War hero Colonel Alexander Doniphan, was founded in 1847. It has been the county seat of Ripley County since that date and was incorporated as a fourth-class city in 1891.

Transportation and Industry • U.S. Highways 160 and 142 and State Highway 21 meet in Doniphan. A railroad constructed in 1883 ceased to operate in 1982, just shy of its centennial. By that time, railroad service had dwindled down to the occasional freight train. In December of that year, when the Current River reached a record flood stage of 27.3 feet, it flooded twenty businesses and damaged fifty-three homes, as well as the railroad line. After the waters receded, it was decided that the railroad would not be repaired. Lumbering and general farming are the primary industries, as well as tourism.

Location • Doniphan is located on the eastern border of the Missouri Ozarks in southeast Missouri, a few miles north of the Arkansas state line, on Current River.

Interesting Facts

*D*oniphan was formerly known as the Railroad Tie Capital of the World. However, when demand for railroad ties dropped, the large railroad tie yard was no longer needed in Doniphan. Today, area sawmills continue to cut ties and truck them out to various area lumberyards.

On September 19, 1864, at the start of Confederate General Sterling Price's Missouri invasion, Union forces burned down the town of Doniphan as an act of retribution. ❧

Trail of Tears

The Nachitoches Trail, also known as the Southwest Trail or the Old Military Road, passes through the county east of Doniphan on its way from Vincennes, Indiana, to Nachitoches, Louisiana. In the winter of 1838, the Benge party of some 1,200 Cherokees traveled down the Old Military Road, making it part of the Trail of Tears. ❧

Garnet Hunt White and Renie Burghardt of Doniphan

Renie Burghardt and Garnet Hunt White enjoy the tranquility Doniphan has to offer. According to Renie, "After having spent vacations in Doniphan and falling in love with the area, I made it my home in 1983. By that time, my children were grown and living their own lives. It was time for me to realize a dream.

"I have never been sorry that I did. The people here are friendly and helpful, the setting is rural and lovely, and the beautiful Current River, winding its way through the area, is the icing on the cake! My children and grandchildren love to come to Doniphan on their vacations, and my friend, Garnet Hunt White, a retired teacher and prominent Doniphan native, quickly became my Doniphan family. Together, we enjoy much of what Doniphan offers its lucky residents." ❧

Local Legend

When the town was being platted, a barrel of whiskey was rolled out and tapped. Once the founding fathers finished their work, they discovered the town had been located sixty feet over an adjoining property line, and that some of the streets intersected at odd angles. ❧

A Wee Gathering

by Sharon Cupp Pennington | *Santa Fe, Texas*

I WILL FOREVER REMEMBER the timbre of the neonatal intensive care unit: flashing lights, the abrasive buzz of an alarm jerking parents to attention, the tentative smiles and collective sighs of relief when it turns out to be nothing, monitors keeping cadence with tiny heartbeats, and respirators circulating life-sustaining air for lungs not yet able to accomplish the task on their own. Every few feet there is another occupied isolette—a regulated and enclosed clear incubator—or a small metal crib. Between these sit haggard mothers or red-vested volunteers, crooning, consoling.

A father rushes in seeking the reassuring glance that will carry him to the end of another workday. A nurse, one of many resident angels, logs in notes at her station. A doctor continues quietly through his morning rounds, here one minute, there the next.

Each one with a story to tell. If there was ever a place filled with more love and faith and courage, determination, and the absolute will to survive, I can't name it.

Life goes on, and love sustains.

My husband sits across from me holding one of the two new additions to our family. He looks at me and I wonder if we're thinking the same thing. Probably not. By the goofy grin on his handsome face, I'm sure he's caught up in the miracle grandbaby in his arms. I'm thinking, *What a year we've had.* First our daughter's difficult conception and pregnancy, then the injuries I suffered in a hit-and-run accident. Two months in the hospital, another five in a wheelchair, and an additional four in rehab. One crisis after another, stripping away the mundane, reminding us of what is truly important.

I glance at the tiny bundle again and blink back tears. But for God's grace, I would've missed all of this.

During my recovery, many people said to me, "There's a reason you didn't die that night." I smile at the memory as I watch one of those reasons cradled in my husband's loving arms. Amid the buzzes and bleeps of life support, I hear him whisper to the fussy infant, "What a big girl you are."

Though she isn't. In all honesty, you could carry this dark-haired beauty in a shoebox. The older of our daughter's twins by a single minute, Sasha Grace entered this world at a wailing, wriggling four pounds, eight ounces. Shane Gabriel weighed in at four pounds, three.

Our family is both lucky and extremely blessed. Born at just under thirty-five weeks, our grandbabies are tiny but healthy—and I'm here to enjoy them. To savor this moment with the man I've loved for so many years, the four of us the only people in the world. To hold these miracle babies and touch them, to teach them that music sounds unbelievably better if you go heavy on the bass and crank up the volume, that rock will always roll, and chocolate-chip cookie dough tastes almost as good as the cookies themselves. Almost. That with folded ribbon, a few ties, and some strategically placed scissor snips, you can create a real bow. That being labeled stubborn is a compliment, and, most importantly, if you can dream and visualize, you can do anything.

Life goes on, and love sustains.

I silently pray that every child in this unit survives, and that each will grow to his or her full potential. For none of these devoted parents to go home empty-handed, empty-hearted.

In a few days, as our babies continue to gain strength and weight, they'll move from their isolettes to the small metal cribs. Then they'll do thirty to forty-five minutes in their infant car seats, a test in preparation for the long ride to their home in Santa Fe, Texas, where they'll be transplanted into a nursery decorated with whimsical carousels, ballerina bunnies, and cowboy bears. And for a while, our world will be immersed in that wonderfully familiar, magical smell only babies possess.

Then they'll grow and graduate, love and marry. They'll have children to raise and worry over, become old, and revel in grandbabies of their own. I wouldn't have missed this for the world, and I'll be eternally grateful I didn't have to. ᥫᦡ

The Prayer Wheel

by Lad Moore | *Altus, Arkansas*

"IT WAS STELL ON THE PHONE AGAIN," my wife explained. "She says she's counting the days until we get there."

Every Thanksgiving was the same. The extended families awaited the call from Granny Stell that told of special plans for the year's most celebratory meal. The conversation always ended the same reassuring way. "No," she would say, "You dare not bring a thing."

It was like a migration of wayward birds returning to their famed Capistrano. From all across the country, family members descended on Hardesty Farm in rural Altus, Arkansas. Early arrivers got the choice bedrooms—the foot-draggers having to settle for cots and pallets. But somehow all the kids made it back—except for the year my brother Jim had his wisdom teeth removed and was sentenced to broth and tepid ice cream for his Thanksgiving Day fare. He didn't make it back.

Those of manly arts persuasion usually enjoyed a day of pheasant hunting in the fields below the grape vineyards. A successful hunt meant that a couple of pheasants would command escort duty on the platter with the Thanksgiving turkey.

Grandpa Hardesty always said grace. It was as if he spent the preceding twelve months keeping notes for just this occasion. He made sure each family member was represented in what we called his prayer wheel—citing an event in our lives during the year. Maybe it was nothing more than little Archie's "C" in arithmetic, or Aunt Flossie's recovery from a bout with the croup. Perhaps it was just thanks for Jim's new job or—ahem—acknowledgment of "Old Maid" Ruth's surprise honeymoon.

We all felt special when Grandpa got to our name in the wheel. Not so much for what he said, but because we knew he had cared enough to keep track of us all for another year. Eventually, Grandpa worked through the entire list—despite the occasional impatient eye that would peek at the waiting vittles and stir a resurgence of salivary juices.

"Amen, great God and Jehovah. Amen."

The blessing was over. Like spontaneous combustion, clangs from the arming of utensils engulfed the room. Grandpa carved the turkey as dervish-like hands passed the platters in both directions. Erupting conversations ran left, right, and sideways. Words and sentences, pent-up from the long prayer, gushed out in unison.

And so we carried on, year after year. One particular Thanksgiving sticks out in my mind, though. After the long prayer wheel concluded, the table erupted into serving and eating. Someone's voice carried loud and clear. "Would you look at these lovely peas!"

Another gave stern directions. "Jaime, take some of this corn. It's Grandpa Hardesty's own."

Aunt Flossie, a proud cook in her own right, offered a veiled challenge. "Stell," she asked, "did you change something in this giblet gravy? Do I taste oregano?"

Occupying a third of my plate were Stell's prize-winning purple-hull peas, slow simmered with bacon, peppers, and a hint of sugar. Stell's rules forbade the buying of shelled peas. Family members earned the right to eat peas by shelling them first. As a child in my summers at Hardesty Farm, we shelled peas together in family ritual.

I remember how Stell formed a bowl in her lap with her apron to cradle the peas. The hulls were tossed onto a newspaper spread on the floor. Guy Lombardo's music paced the activity, his sounds wandering our way from a giant Philco radio that was the nesting place for Grandpa's aromatic pipe tobaccos.

To sop up the pot liquor, there was scalded cornbread emblazoned with shards of cayenne peppers. To help tame it, it received a cardio-risky triple patty of butter.

We heaped our plates with turkey and sage dressing, along with mayonnaise-drenched salad. The delicate flowers on Stell's best china were completely obscured by the overhang of double helpings.

For dessert there were the Thanksgiving Trinity pies—pecan, pumpkin, and lemon icebox. As a special temptation, Stell had also prepared the same coconut cake that once earned her a blue ribbon at the Ozark Fair. It was special because she grated a fresh coconut herself—merging it into a secret-ingredient icing. It was also her custom—I never knew its origin—to hide a dime somewhere in the cake. Whoever found it presumably would have good luck.

Everyone took a piece, but with the first bite, we all stopped chewing. Large chunks fell from wide-open mouths. The cake held the unmistakable taste of soap! All conversation stopped, the soft radio music coming from the living room heard for the first time that day.

Stell first objected, then denied. She got up quickly and went over to the sink, where the coconut still lay. Missing was the big bar of Ivory soap from its place on the dish above the faucet. Her face was ablaze with embarrassment.

"Oh my stars . . ." she said under her breath.

Each of us in turn used humor to lighten our reaction.

"That doesn't compare with the time Grandpa forgot to remove the pellets from those pheasants," I said, "Near 'bout broke my only gold tooth!"

"Remember when Aunt Flossie made that upside-down cake that Jaime said he couldn't tell up from down?" asked Jim.

Eventually, we pried a smile from Stell's embarrassed lips. Even Flossie showed restraint over the champion cook's error, but I noticed a hit of satisfaction in her partial smile. The rest of us just smiled, already looking forward to next Thanksgiving. Grandpa had been seen making a note of the event. It would undoubtedly reappear somewhere in next year's wheel.

Oh—and, in all the fuss, nobody found the dime.

Home on the Lake

by Kristin Dreyer Kramer | *Baldwin, Michigan*

I WAS FOUR YEARS OLD when my parents bought a cottage on a small lake in Northern Michigan. It was just a tiny one-bedroom cabin, but it quickly became our home away from home—my family's favorite retreat.

Mom and Dad, my two older brothers, and I spent many summer weekends at the cottage. Even when my brothers got part-time jobs, we worked around their schedules—often loading up the car and leaving on our two-hour drive to the cottage as soon as they got home from work on Friday night.

On Saturdays, we spent the day splashing around in the water and speeding across the lake in our boat, our hair getting lighter and lighter as the summer months passed, and our skin growing darker and darker. At night, we ate burgers at the picnic table and spent time together around the campfire, chatting and joking, and accidentally burning marshmallows.

On Sundays, we fought over the one tiny bathroom and sat together on metal folding chairs for church in the little chapel down the path. We spent the afternoon on the beach or napping in the cottage. We stayed out of the water, and the boat stayed tied to the dock—none of that was allowed on Sunday.

Grandpa and Grandma often joined us on our summer weekends at the cottage. Grandpa spent the afternoons relaxing in the shade, cheering me on and waving as I performed my aquatic acrobatics. And Grandma loved to sit at the little kitchen table at night and on rainy afternoons, laughing and playing cards.

It was great to have them visit, but the most exciting time of the summer—maybe even the whole year—was the Fourth of July. That was when the whole family showed up—Mom and Dad, Grandpa and Grandma, my brothers, two uncles, two aunts, three cousins, and me. The cottage swelled with excitement on the weekend of the Fourth. There were always kids in the lake. Someone was always on skis behind the boat, and there was always plenty of potato salad and burgers and fresh watermelon for everyone. To me, it was just as exciting as Christmas—the smell of the grill, the constant noise of conversation, the whole family squeezing in wherever they could.

At night on the Fourth, the guys made a fire and we all gathered on the beach to "ooh" and "aah" over the fireworks while dancing in the cool beach sand with bright-colored sparklers. We made s'mores as we laughed and cheered, and picked our favorites. My little cousin, Amber, and I would try to guess which color would come next.

When the show was over and the marshmallow bag empty, Amber and I were tucked into bed in the cottage's only bedroom. We whispered until we fell asleep to the sound of giggling aunts and a high-energy card game. When it was finally time for the adults to go to sleep, they carefully moved us to the enclosed porch, where we woke up on Sunday morning to the smell of bacon and eggs, surrounded by kids in sleeping bags sharing pull-out couches.

It's been years since all of us last gathered at the cottage to celebrate the Fourth of July. Grandpa and Grandma no longer play cards by the kitchen table or enjoy the shade of their favorite chairs, and

I've since moved away from home. But whenever I come home for a visit, there's nothing I love more than driving up to the cottage.

A new family gathers there now. My niece and nephew are the ones splashing in the water, giggling with their grandpa and grandma, eating watermelon and burgers, and watching the fireworks on the Fourth. Someday, maybe, my kids will join them in their sleeping bags on the porch, and they'll grow up with the same wonderful memories as I have.∽

Then There Were Six

by Betty Downs | *Clyde, North Dakota*

IN THE WINTER OF 1945, World War II was winding down when the telegram from my brother Roy arrived. It read: Discharged December 21, Home for Christmas. We hadn't seen Roy since he left for the army in July of 1942.

Bob, my oldest brother, had enlisted in the Army before Pearl Harbor, and he had been discharged earlier that fall. He had served at air bases in England during the war, while Roy spent most of his time fighting in the South Pacific. The telegram from Ft. Lewis gave hope this would be the first time in five years our family of six would be together for Christmas.

On December 22, a severe snowstorm enveloped the prairie. Dad paced the floor and listened to radio reports on KDLR Devils Lake. Mother busied herself in the kitchen baking "snooze" cookies, and angel food cake, favorites of our returning soldiers. Walter, another brother who would serve his country later, and I kept busy playing cards.

By noon on Christmas Eve, the storm had abated. Dad, his face grim, came into the kitchen to announce the latest road report. "The railroad track between here and Devils Lake is blocked. The boy won't be able to get home."

Somber silence was broken when Bob said, "Heck, I'll drive to Devils Lake in the car and pick him up."

Dad looked doubtful. "The highway is blocked too. You won't be able to get through, and we aren't even sure he'll be on the train today."

Walter piped up, "Hey, I've got a date tonight, I need the car!"

"Sorry brother," said Bob. "I'm taking the car, and you're going with me."

Heavy coats, mittens, and warm caps were donned. "Don't forget the shovels," Dad called.

Devils Lake was 50 miles south of our farm. *It could be a long time before I see any of my brothers,* I thought, as I watched the red tail-lights of the Model A Ford disappear into the slowly drifting snow. I watched the car bounce over snow packed roads until it faded away into the early winter dusk.

Waiting for brothers to come home from a long war seemed like a piece of cake compared to the sentimentality I now had to endure. I thought of all the V-Mails we had written and waited for, the war pictures we had watched when we went to the movie theater, and the fear that clutched our insides when we read of the air strikes in Europe or the battles that took place on Iwo Jima and in the Philippines. Then, my heartbeat quickening, I pictured Bob and Walter sitting in a cold car stuck in a snowdrift on Christmas Eve, and Roy stranded in a train depot, lonely and alone one more Christmas Day.

Later that evening, KDLR reported that Highway 20 had been opened north of Starkweather. Hope flickered in Dad's eyes. Starkweather was a little town between the farm and Devils Lake. Hours passed, and at about 10 P.M., lights illumined our snowy driveway.

In a rush of adrenaline, Mother called, "It's them! It's the boys."

And she and Dad ran to the dark window to see if the car held two or hopefully three passengers.

I dropped the Christmas angel I had been hanging on the tree and ran through the big dining room just as the door opened. Pandemonium and shouts of joy filled our house as Roy's manly figure filled the doorway. My lanky seventeen-year-old body jumped up over the kitchen chair and I fell into the arms of a brother I hadn't laid eyes on for three and a half years. Tears of surprise filled his eyes as he recognized his "Sis," who had been a short, thirteen-year-old tomboy when he left.

Later, over hot chocolate, we heard the story.

After shoveling their way through many packed drifts to reach their destination, the boys arrived tired and anxious at the train depot in Devils Lake, soon after the train had arrived from the west. Not knowing for sure if Roy was even on that train, Bob boarded the passenger car to search for his brother while Walter talked to the conductor. In the meantime, Roy was already in the depot learning that the train north, to Christmas and home, would not be running that night. Just as he was debating his options, he turned. Miraculously, there were his two brothers.

Roy chuckled, but his eyes sparkled with misty tears. "They were a sight for sore eyes."

These days, whenever I think of Christmas and time spent together, I remember the snowstorm of 1945, and a family gathering that could never be matched.

Wishbone Science

by N.V. Bennett | *Sun Prairie, Montana*

IT WAS A COLD AND WINDY FALL DAY as we stepped onto the frozen road in our itchy Sunday best. Most Sundays we would have whined, but on certain occasions, when that special aroma wafted from the stovepipes straight to our noses, we were too excited to protest. Instead, we raced across the winding roads to our grandparent's house for dinner, autumn leaves swirling around our feet as we ran. With the onset of darkness, cornstalks left standing in the fields swayed ominously, crackling in the gusty breezes and sounding like the rustle of wild animals. Undeterred, we hurried on, for the wind also carried the smell of Grandmother's turkey.

The meal itself was always a grand affair: roast corn, oozing with butter; mashed potatoes—skins off for special occasions; dill and sweet pickles of all sorts and sizes; white rolls and tons of gravy; and, of course, mushed-up turnip for my mother and grandmother.

The turkey made a resounding thump as it was hoisted from the stove to the table. And when Grandfather began to carve, the juices flowed down and across the blue serving plate. We salivated like dogs in anticipation.

Because I was his favorite, Grandfather always saved the wishbone for me.

The science of wishbone preparation was no simple matter. You couldn't take a fresh one and make your wish right then and there. You had to age it first. That meant drying it carefully, turning it daily, and not forgetting it on the pantry shelf or fridge top. Timing was everything. Too long and it would shard off—you would have trouble making a clear break. Too soft and it would be rubbery, twisty, and no matter how hard you tried you could not bend it to break properly.

There was also the important choice of the right partner to break it with. My parents rarely participated. Mom thought the idea was paramount to germ spreading, a regular Typhoid Mary in the making. If she found my wishbone, it would end up in the garbage can, and I would have to wait till the next turkey dinner and then hide it better.

Grandfather was a sport, but he had tough gnarled sailor fingers, which sometimes didn't fit, and Grandmother's blue veined knitting hands were too busy for games. This left me with my siblings to choose from.

Diplomacy dictated that I ask Cathy, the eldest sister, first. I was glad when she said no, for she did not present much of a partner. She neither believed nor disbelieved in such things as luck and wishbones. Who would want to share a wishbone and possibly a wish with a disbeliever?

My second eldest sister was Pat. I often didn't bother to ask her, either. Pat simply couldn't be bothered—too busy with boys or dreaming of rock stars—and she hated turkey.

Brother Ken was to be avoided at all costs. I hid my precious wishbone if I saw him coming. He would twist my arm in half as well as the wishbone, and if I refused to hand it over or say "Uncle" he might give me a snake bite.

That left the next in line: Jeanette. She was still of an age where she believed in wishbones, good luck charms, and giving a smaller, younger sister a fair chance by using her weaker hand.

Now, with a family of my own, I have become the cooker of the turkey. My husband does the oven calculations and carves the sacred bird.

Perhaps I have grown too old for childish wishes; perhaps by now I might have other bones to pick. But I still remember Grandpa, who was never too old for magic, and so each time I cook a turkey, I secret away the wishbone and wrap it in a clean paper towel. After it dries, I summon my daughters to join fingers, close their eyes, and pull in hopes of a clean break and the chance to wish. ᐤᐤ

The Gathering Place

by Betty R. Koffman | *St. Paul, Virginia*

"JUST A COUPLE MORE HILLS," I said to my husband as we passed through the small Virginia town of St. Paul, on a hot Sunday in August. I pointed to a dot on the map. "Here we are, and here's Dry Fork."

Kim nodded. "I'm not driving all this way without finding it."

I grinned at him. I didn't plan on turning around until I'd found it, either. We were in search of an old hillside cemetery where my great-grandfather, a Confederate veteran of the Civil War, was buried. Armed with only the name of the community and some vague memories from the last time I was there, which had been more than forty years ago, we had left Tennessee behind and driven through beautiful Virginia farm country.

My great-grandfather Henry Robinett was a descendant of Allyn Robinett and Margaret Sym, who married in London around 1652 and later emigrated to the United States. Henry was born in 1843 in Wise County, deep in southwestern Virginia. When the Civil War began in 1861, Henry was hardly more than a boy, the son of a farmer, and according to family lore, one of the first in the county to join the Confederate army.

He served in the Seventh Virginia Cavalry Battalion, a unit active in Kentucky, West Virginia, and Saltville, Virginia, where they fought the Yankees who had come to destroy the salt works. In an interview with a local newspaper in 1938, when Henry was in his nineties, he recalled many skirmishes in Kentucky and up at Saltville.

After the war ended, Henry farmed and hauled freight by wagon into Kentucky and the Carolinas and as far as Lynchburg, Virginia, returning with goods to sell at home. Uncle Henry, as he was known, loved to wrestle and to dance the pigeon wing, even in old age, and claimed he'd marry again if he could find a good woman. He died in 1943 at the age of 100, leaving behind 200 descendants.

I checked the map again as the road began to descend down the mountain. When I glanced up again, there was a small sign by the road announcing we had arrived at our destination.

"There it is, Dry Fork. Turn left here."

I tried to remember more details, but failed. I remembered a house on a bank above the road, a flight of steep stone steps, and across the road a slope that dropped off to a creek. We had to find those steps.

After about a mile, the road forked, and we turned right. Off to our left, below the road, was the creek I remembered. We were getting close. I was sure of it. I felt a fluttering in my stomach, but we saw no steps. After a couple of miles, I said, "We've gone too far."

Kim raised his eyebrows. "You're sure?" We headed back a ways.

Spotting a family in the parking lot of a small church, I motioned with my hand toward them. "Let's stop and ask."

The man we asked happened to be a Wise County deputy sheriff. When I explained what we were looking for, he nodded. "Is that the old man who was in the Civil War?" When I answered yes, he moved toward his vehicle. "Follow us."

Within minutes, the car in front of us slowed. As we watched, the sheriff stuck an arm out of the window and waved toward the bank. There, almost completely hidden by grass and vines, was the set of nearly vertical stone steps I remembered. Above the road sat the white house. Excited now, I waved my thanks to the deputy, and he and his family drove on.

We parked across the road and hauled ourselves up the steps, grasping clumps of grass. Kim reached the top, gave me a hand, and pulled me up. We pushed forward, through a stand of saplings, and into a clearing. I stared disappointedly at the neglected cemetery, now immersed in deep weeds. It had been a while since anyone had mowed. But in that split second, I could almost see my family caretaking there, all those years ago, laughing and talking as we cut and stacked brush to burn.

In an instant, it all came back. I recalled one eventful cleaning day when my father picked up a pile of brush in which a copperhead lay entangled. I remembered how my mother's shriek had echoed across the valley.

For a moment, I just stood there trying to get my bearings. I could see graves, but somehow I knew Henry's was farther up the hillside. We stepped cautiously through knee-deep grasses and a tangle of weeds, hot and sweaty in jeans and boots. I stopped to catch my breath, wiped perspiration from my forehead, and determinedly moved forward, following my instincts. As we passed a spreading maple tree, I saw it, the steeple on the small marble monument, strangely clean and white in the sunlight, surrounded by others gray with dirt. A few of the tombstones lay toppled on the ground, but not my great-grandfather's.

Below a Confederate cross was carved HENRY ROBINETTE, 7 VIRGINIA CAVALRY. No date of birth or death was given. I knelt to take photographs and suddenly felt a swelling in my chest at the distant memories of family gathered, on this very spot, and the connection that remains no matter how far in time we come from our forebears.

Nearby lay one of Henry's sons, my grandfather, a twin who had died in Tennessee in the 1940s, and one of his wives, my grandmother, who died when my father was a mere child of ten. Three links in a family chain.

We stayed awhile, resting in the shade of that peaceful place, with only the quiet rush of cars on the road below, and the whisper of the hot breeze in the treetops. Later, as we made our way down, I turned to look back and fancied I could hear the voices of my parents, and my brother and sister—all the other relatives who had worked side by side so long ago to keep the woods from reclaiming the old burial ground.

A faint smile touched my face. Without thought, my hand moved to my lips and I blew a kiss to the spirits of my family who had gathering atop this lonely hill. Some were free to come and go at will; others would remain here forever. As the breezes chased one another across the land, ruffling the tall grasses, I realized that no matter where I might live, or how many miles I might travel, this gathering place would always hold a very special place in my heart.⌒

Hearthstone Halloween

by Mary Helen Straker (as told by her Aunt Emma) | *Whigville, Ohio*

AS THE LAST OF HER FAMILY, Aunt Emma had priceless memories. In her final years, she loved to reminisce and talk of her early life, shared by my mother. One day I asked her about the Halloweens of her childhood, celebrated at her grandparents' house near the small southeastern Ohio town of Whigville, in Noble County. This is how she told it.

In 1900, the Guilers gathered at the family hearth to celebrate Halloween. It was an annual event, the ritual unchanging.

Samuel Guiler, my grandfather, forked a hot potato from the fireplace, flicked off the ashes and split it open onto the warm plate his wife, Caroline, handed him.

In went sweet, fresh-churned butter—a sizeable chunk. Samuel took an egg from a basket and broke it into the steaming potato. He fork-whipped it into the thick, mealy contents, sprinkled it with salt and handed it to his daughter, Mary. Back he went to the fireplace for another potato, repeating the process until all were served.

As Samuel doled out potatoes, Caroline passed a pitcher of celery, crisping in ice water—a rare treat—to the family group. My parents, siblings, aunts, uncles, and cousins gathered around the hearth to observe the tradition. Grown-ups sat on settles and rocking chairs while the children hunkered down on hooked rugs scattered over the handwoven carpet.

The big fireplace was used for cooking as well as heat. The meat spit hung at the top, and from it was suspended the wrought-iron pan of apples filled with brown sugar and butter, which sizzled and sputtered over the banked fire and perfumed the air with sweet spice.

Caroline dished up the fruit, poured on thick, heavy cream, and passed it along. Mouths watered, waiting, before each spoon dipped into the rich syrupy juice.

After the meal, and by popular demand, Samuel recited the poem "Tam O'Shanter," by Robert Burns. He knew all nineteen verses from memory, and rolled his r's beautifully. A born performer, Samuel was actually a son of Erin, just one generation removed from the old sod. Of commanding stature, his wavy white hair was profuse, as were his beard and mustache, and Samuel wielded his cane like a royal scepter.

Finished with the poem, he took out his kerchief and wiped his brow.

"Satisfied now, are ye? Sufficient for one evenin'?"

"No, no, PaPaw. The Red Shoes story!" the children demanded.

"Well, then," he answered. "If you persist. Here's how it came about."

In the year of 1804, an Irish couple, finding themselves the objects of religious persecution in their homeland, resolved to take themselves and their daughter—a wee, toddling child—to America. Prior to boarding the ship in Dublin, they stayed the night with friends, who gave the little girl a pair of red shoes.

On board the ship, preparing to set sail, the mother discovered the shoes to be missing, left behind at the house of their friends.

The child wailed piteously, "My shoes. My shoes," as if her small heart would break.

The father, being assured he had time before the ship's departure, went back for the shoes, returning only to find the ship well on its way down the harbor. He leaped into a rowboat in hot pursuit. Alas, to no avail! Back at the dock he learned he had to wait two weeks for another ship bound for New York. He waited two weeks and boarded the ship, but early in the voyage, it was overtaken by a British man o'war, who seized our hero and a number of his compatriots and pressed them into service aboard the British vessel.

After weeks and months of forced duty on the high seas, in the winter of 1805, the men were happy to learn that the ship was docking in the port of Halifax, in Nova Scotia. In the night, six of the men contrived to escape, sliding down a rope into the icy water. They separated. Our hero lost his companion and struggled through the night alone, his clothes frozen to his body.

When, at last, he reached the limit of his endurance, he saw a light, crawled toward it, and collapsed upon the doorstep of a lonely cabin. Its inhabitants nursed him back to health until spring, when he was able to make his way to the coast and take passage on a ship to New York.

He combed the streets of the city, searching for his lost loved ones. To subsist, he took work in a tailor shop. Throughout the summer he searched, fruitlessly. One evening, in the late fall of '06, worn out from work and disheartened, he found his way into a poor common eating house, where he set about to purchase his supper. As he sat at the table, he pulled a bag from his pocket and removed the wee shoes, carried upon his person throughout the hazardous, lengthy journey. He set the shoes on the table and sat pondering them with tears in his eyes.

So lost in misery was he that he was unaware of someone approaching, until a child's voice exclaimed, "My shoes! My shoes!" His heart lurched in his throat. He looked up to regard the child—and to look into the face of the woman following, the face of his own true wife.

The child was my sister, now departed this life. For the man, you see, the man was my father.❧

THE TOWN OF
Whigville, Ohio
Population: 17

Town Facts

Original name • The town of Whigville was originally called Freedom. The name was officially changed to Whigville on March 10, 1891, by an act of the Ohio Legislature.

Location • Whigville, a hamlet in Marion Township, located in Noble County in southeastern Ohio, was laid out in 1846 on hilly land about 10 miles east of Caldwell, the county seat.

Interesting places • In addition to the blacksmith shop, which dates to 1832, early structures include a frame store, a church with an adjacent cemetery, and a one-room schoolhouse. The church, St. Paul's Methodist Episcopal, was first built in 1837 and rebuilt in 1866. The church closed for services in the 1950s, and in 1982, the Methodist church authorized the removal of its stained-glass windows and pews for use in a new church elsewhere. A concerned group—not all with Whigville connections—raised the money to purchase the church and the original windows, and provided the church with new pews and railings. Now fully restored and renamed the Whigville Community Church, the white frame building is home to regular services. It stands today as it has for 167 years, a landmark on the crest of the hill on the main street of the town.

Industry and Transportation

Wheat, tobacco, and hogs and cattle were early enterprises. Beginning in 1853, the Central Ohio Railroad provided access to eastern markets. In those early years, it took a bushel of wheat to buy a pound of coffee, and a farm laborer earned eight dollars a month or split rails at thirty-one cents per hundred.

On August 1, 1883, the Bellaire, Zanesville, and Cincinnati, a narrow gauge railroad, completed its track through Whigville to Summerfield. Called "Bent, Zigzag, and Crooked," by the local people, the BZ&C continued to Zanesville later that year, opening new worlds to its customers. In 1886, Whigville, with a population of seventy-one, was a flag stop. The station was located inside a general store.

The three-foot-wide track (the standard was four feet) wound through the scenic hills of southeastern Ohio on 300 trestles and bridges. The tallest trestle was 55 feet high. Mudslides were common, and with flimsily built tracks, the train was accident-prone. The worst train wreck occurred April 5, 1895, when the train derailed and demolished the "jumbo" trestle west of Whigville.

Never a profitable venture, the BZ&C came out of bankruptcy in July, 1902, reborn as the Ohio River and Western Railroad. The OR&W ran until 1931, making its last trip on Memorial Day, May 30, of that year. ❧

The Guilers of Whigville

There were once a number of Mary Helen Straker's relatives in Whigville. She writes, "As a child, my mother often visited her stepmother's parents, Caroline and Samuel Guiler, on their farm near Whigville. It was there, with my aunt, her half sister, that Mother heard the red shoes story. My father and his eight siblings were born and grew up on a farm near Whigville. My paternal great-grandparents are buried in the cemetery there. Last Memorial Day, my cousin, a Guiler great-granddaughter, showed me the site of the Guiler farm down the hill from the church and on a side road. No trace of the farm remains today." ❧

Christmas at Napoleon

by Linda Kaullen Perkins | *Napoleon, Missouri*

"Napoleon, Missouri, population 215," Daddy announced.

Mama looked over her shoulder at me in the back seat, her face stern. "Now, Linda Kay, I want you to be on your best behavior. Play nice with your cousins because you know who comes tonight."

"Santa Claus!" I shouted.

"That's right, now sit back down and don't get your dress wrinkled."

My heart pounded as Daddy eased the lime-green, 1950 Chevy down the steep hill leading to Grandma's house. I hung on, legs straight out, bracing my feet against the back of Daddy's seat, and tried not to think about the deep ravine or the sharp curve at the bottom of the hill. What if Daddy's foot slipped off the brake and we plunged over the railroad tracks, straight into the river? I held my breath as we crept around the curve.

Three houses came into sight, all within shouting distance of one another. Our seventy-two-mile journey had ended safely. Tonight we would celebrate Christmas Eve, 1955.

As we pulled into the driveway, Grandpa appeared from the brown tar-paper house, followed by four of my jumping and shouting cousins. Butch, my wildest cousin, sprinted to his gray house and, with a puff of white breath, yelled, "They're here, they're here!"

My cousin, Donna, ran to the white house, shouting, "Come on out!" Within minutes, five adults and four children stood beside our car, peering in the windows.

"Get out, Blue-eyed Blondie," Grandpa said. I stumbled out, snuggling into his bear hug.

Uncle Chee stepped on his cigarette before taking Mama's overnight case from her. Aunt Frances kissed me, and then picked up Mama's grocery bag filled with cartons of cookies. Uncle Charles helped Daddy lift the big suitcase out of the turtle shell.

My oldest cousin, Roy, carried Mama's Woolworth's shopping bag stuffed with Christmas gifts. "Here's one with my name," he shouted.

Grandma flung open the kitchen door and we were enveloped by the smell of baking bread. She hugged and kissed me as I eyed the four apple pies lining the kitchen counter. "Come in the living room," she said, her brown eyes snapping.

Diane, my youngest cousin, grabbed my hand. "Wait till you see Grandma's tree. Donna and I just added paper chains."

The scent of cedar filled the living room. Twinkling in the corner, taller than the biggest giant in a fairy tale, stood the Christmas tree, its limbs laden with glass balls, silver icicles, paper ornaments, and popcorn strings.

"Ooooh," I murmured.

As Mama added our gifts to the growing mountain, my insides jiggled with excitement and I hugged my arms over my stomach.

"You must be hungry," Aunt Phyllis said, her hand squeezing my shoulder. Before long, we kids were sitting down to eat at a card table near the Christmas tree. As we ate, my cousins planned.

"Tonight," Donna said, "we'll do the dishes."

"Yep," Diane nodded.

I frowned. "Why?"

"Because," Donna whispered, "we'll get to open presents sooner."

After the last bite of apple pie, Roy announced, "Us kids will do the dishes."

With globs of suds, Butch and Donna washed. Roy handled Grandma's silver teakettle, pouring scalding water over soapy dishes, and Diane and I dried. Soon, a pile of clean Blue Willow dishes had grown on the oak table.

Grandma glanced over our shoulders. "Go on, kids. Get to passin' out presents."

I had five. Grandma and Grandpa gave me two of the most important things they thought I needed: a Bible and a teddy bear. My cousins gave me a coloring book, crayons, a fuzzy wind-up dog, and modeling clay.

After we had opened up the presents, Uncle Charles announced, "Time to go home," and not one of my cousins argued. Not on Christmas Eve.

The next day everyone came back for Christmas dinner, and everything was perfect—until that afternoon.

"Diane," I said, "let's take your new piano into the bedroom."

"Okay," she said, following me.

She set it on the white, chenille bedspread and pounded out a tin-like tune. I pretended to be interested in the new doll Santa had brought.

"I know how to play 'Chopsticks,'" I said, edging closer. "Can I show you?"

"No," she said as she continued punching the keys.

"Come on, let me play it."

"No," she said a little louder.

"If you don't let me play your piano," I paused long enough to think up a good threat, "I'm going to bite your nose."

She shook her head back and forth, her curls bouncing. "No!"

Before I had thought it all out, I grabbed her and made good my promise.

"Ow!" she shrieked. Holding her hand over her face, she ran into the living room wailing. "Linda Kay bit me on the nose!"

"Wait!" I yelled, close on her heels, my heart pounding.

When I burst into the living room, I froze. Conversation stopped, and all eyes turned in my direction. Uncle Chee smashed out his cigarette. Aunt Frances's beautiful eyes searched my face. Grandpa said "Tsk, tsk," before looking at Daddy. Daddy nodded at Mama. Fear slid up my spine. What had I done?

"Linda Kay." Mama's voice quivered. "Come into the bedroom with me right now!"

I slunk behind her, dragging the toes of my saddle oxfords.

She pulled the folding door shut, leading me to the corner. "What is the matter with you? Why would you do such a thing? I'm ashamed of you, Linda Kay."

My heart sank. I felt as bad as if I had broken Grandma's entire set of Blue Willow dishes. Now, everyone knew I was naughty.

Mama marched past me and yanked open the door. "Come in here, Diane."

Diane came in, rubbing her nose and sniffing way too loudly.

"Go on, Linda." Mama clamped her hand on my shoulder. "What do you have to say?"

"I'm sorry, Diane," I said, bursting into tears.

Though the naughty streak I had when I was a young girl is long gone, on occasion, Diane still asks, "Do you remember the time ..." Unfortunately, I do remember—but in my defense, it was the first and last time I ever bit anyone!

The Sugar-Cube Cure

by Cheryl K. Pierson | *Sissonville, West Virginia*

JALAPEÑO PEPPERS WERE HARD TO FIND in Sissonville, West Virginia, but my brother-in-law, Tom, had mentioned that he'd like some "real" south-of-the-border cuisine. Having traveled the United States as a long-haul truck driver, Tom knew the difference between a real enchilada and one that was merely a cheap imitation. I figured if I could find the canned ingredients, I might be able to manage something in between.

I knew all about Mexican food. A transplanted Oklahoman, I had discovered years earlier that, although there were wonderful Italian restaurants in the West Virginian neck of the woods, Mexican eateries were scarcer than the proverbial hen's teeth.

I had grown up in the Southwest with the spicy meats that filled tacos, enchiladas, and tamales, salsa that set your ears smoking, and Mexican rice that caused your eyes to water. I loved it, and Tom was a kindred soul.

"Cheryl," he said in his Appalachian drawl, "if you'll make it, I'll buy everything you need."

That Saturday morning, Tom's wife, Prenny, and I set out for Charleston to find the needed goods. Although the chain supermarket boasted of "Mexican food" in the international foods aisle, compared to their Oklahoma counterparts, they were meagerly supplied. But, no matter, I thought, glancing over the few cans of enchilada sauce, refried beans, and tortillas. We would prevail. I spied only one jar of jalapeño peppers and grabbed it up. At the same time, Prenny put three huge packages of meat into our basket.

"That'll be too much," I said.

She smiled. "You never know who might show up. We better buy extra just in case." She reached for another package of tortillas and two more cans of enchilada sauce.

By the time we returned from our shopping excursion, I had begun to wonder if Prenny knew something about this little fiesta of ours that I did not. Four additional cars were parked in front of the house, and people were spilling out onto the front porch—people I didn't even know. "Oh, gosh," Prenny said. I could tell she was not surprised.

As we entered through the garage, I overheard Tom say, "Come on over. Cheryl's cooking Mexican food." He hung up the phone, took the bag of groceries from my arms, and set it on the countertop, and winked. "Might be a few extra people show up." To Tom, everyone was family.

Prenny and I began to cook, and the doorbell began to ring. What had started off as a Mexican dinner for eight people had turned into a buffet. Needing reinforcements, we soon enlisted the help of Prenny's daughters, Linda and Sandy.

There was no hope that we could all sit down to eat together, but the men rounded up every folding chair that side of the Kanawha River and makeshift tables were set up around the house. Before all was said and done, everyone had found a place to sit and had a full plate in front of them.

And still, they came.

From the kitchen, Prenny and I would glance out, see another car filled with family and friends pull up, and return to our task. As the afternoon wore on, we created a Mexican feast worthy of remembrance. It wasn't long before we were out of chips, and running low on salsa. The soda had been the first casualty. We were all drinking water now.

Frank, another brother-in-law, showed up just as we set the next batch of food on the table. Frank, being a man of size, helped himself to everything.

"I love spicy food," he said as he added another spoonful of Mexican rice to his plate. "The hotter, the better!"

Prenny and I offered a weary smile of appreciation before heading back toward the kitchen. We'd been cooking for two hours already, and had served thirty people, yet there was no end in sight. When someone asked us when we were going to hold our next Mexican feast, the question fell on deaf ears.

All at once, the table conversation began to quiet. We heard a muffled sound. Collectively, we turned to see Frank take his napkin and dab at the sudden sweat standing out on his forehead, his face flushed. He grabbed his glass of water and downed it in one huge gulp.

"My ... gosh ...that's ...HOT!"

His eyes watered. He motioned for another glass of something—anything—to quench the fire.

Being used to eating spicy food, I couldn't resist the temptation to have a little fun. I spooned some of the rice into a small bowl, and took a bite. Hot! Just the way I liked it.

I glanced over at Frank and watched him gulp down another glass of water.

"Mmm, this is good." I said as I swallowed another heaping mouthful. I frowned and looked up at my brother-in-law with puzzled eyes. "Frank, what's wrong with this?"

He watched, waiting for it to hit me, waiting for the sweat to break out, the fiery burning to begin, the smoke to come roiling from my ears.

He waited in vain.

Tom grinned as I set the now empty bowl on the table, sharing the joke. Then he helped cool the fire in Frank's mouth with an immediate remedy: a sugar cube.

"Cheryl," Tom drawled, "I think you better teach old Frank here how to say 'the hotter, the better' in Spanish." ❧

A Recipe for Success

by Lisa Ciriello | *Lawton, Oklahoma*

I WAS NEVER ONE OF THOSE PEOPLE who knew from childhood exactly what they wanted to do with their lives.

I grew up observing my brother play "cops and robbers" as a young boy, graduating to "detective" as a pre-teen, and then suddenly I was at his police academy graduation watching him accept his badge and shake the hand of our police commissioner. He just knew from the start that his calling was to protect and serve.

My sister had the voice of an angel. It is said within our family that her first words were uttered in song. She sang in every school holiday pageant since kindergarten, and now makes her living as a vocal coach and part-time studio backup singer.

I was more of a free spirit when it came to mapping out my future. It wasn't a lack of ambition so much as a lack of direction. My interests were varied, yet I just didn't think I was particularly gifted in any one area.

Over the course of our childhood, one of the things my siblings and I did have in common was the anticipation of the holiday season each year at Aunt B's. Christmas dinner always took place at our aunt's home because she was the only family member who had a house large enough to accommodate our family—plus, she was the only female member of our clan with an ounce of domestication.

I remember crossing the threshold of Aunt B's front door every Christmas and being assaulted by the combined warm smells of brown sugar, cinnamon, and chocolate. I can still feel the gravitational pull of her kitchen as we passed right by the tree, surrounded by beautifully wrapped gifts bearing our names, in order to grab a cookie straight from the oven. Our faces bore a mixture of sheer bliss and pure agony as we ate and practically swallowed whole the molten-hot cookies. For days, I tongued the blisters on the roof of my mouth and ruminated about the events of the day: "The Twelve Days of Christmas" sing-along, complete with illustrations by my brother and assigned singing parts—everyone dreaded the part for "*Five golden rings*"; Celtic music wafting through the house, courtesy of my Irish grandfather; the absolute chaos that ensued when you mixed ten children and four dogs with a pile of Christmas presents; and, of course, "the cookie."

One cookie in particular that Aunt B made was simply known as "the cookie." This oatmeal cookie recipe was customized to suit each family member's tastes, and a batch was baked especially for each of us. My brother liked chocolate chunks and coconut in his. My mother preferred raisins and almonds, and while my grandparents were oatmeal cookie purists, I asked for "the works," which included everything but the kitchen sink. These unique treats made us all feel very special.

After college, I took several jobs in the financial, technical, and administrative fields. I worked hard and made a good living, but I never considered myself a success or felt any passion for the work I did. On occasion, I expressed my feelings of discontent to my family, and they gave me varying pieces of advice. The one that always stood out in my mind came from Aunt B, who told me simply that if I was patient I'd eventually find my way ... or it would find me.

A few years ago, Aunt B passed on and left a little something to each one of her family members. I was surprised and quite perplexed to find that she'd left me her recipe for "the cookie." Although I'd spent hours at a time in my aunt's kitchen watching intently as she created one scrumptious cookie after another, I'd never actually baked anything myself.

To honor my aunt and her gift to me, I hosted the next Christmas dinner and gave the recipe a try. I baked each family member's version of the cookie, as well as new versions for the next generation of nieces, nephews, and grandchildren. With an overwhelming sense of satisfaction, I watched my nephews sneak piping hot cookies from the pan, and I listened to my brother and sister reminisce about holidays past and tell their kids stories about Aunt B's kitchen as they ate their versions of the cookie. I realized then that baking for my family brought a feeling of accomplishment and a sense of nurturing that I'd never felt before.

I baked virtually non-stop after that day. Now, several years later, I am the owner of a thriving baking business that brings me the feeling of success and passion for what I do that I'd always hoped for. I thought I was one of those people who would always question her path in life, yet the answer was right in front of me every year in my Aunt B's kitchen.✄

Summertime

by Marcia Rudoff | *Asbury Park, New Jersey*

SUMMER BEGAN WITH THE ARRIVAL OF THE AUNTS, with wiggly cousins firmly in tow and uncles lagging behind, dragging luggage. The aunts and cousins would stay until Labor Day. The uncles would return home and visit on weekends. The aunts were city people, eager to exchange the July and August heat of New York City for the seashore breezes of Asbury Park, New Jersey, my childhood home.

Aunt Rose and my cousin Marilyn stayed with my family. The money Aunt Rose gave my mother helped with the food bills, a real boon since we were surviving the Great Depression by the barter system, exchanging my father's accounting expertise for the products and services of his clients. Unfortunately, none of them were grocers.

Aunt Julie and my cousins, Bennett, David, and Johnny, took rooms nearby. They often joined us for meals and stayed late into the evening, the grown-ups gossiping on the porch while the children chased fireflies.

For several summers of my early childhood, the aunts and cousins became part of our household. Their arrival announced it was, indeed, summer, and the house filled with the sounds of conversation, tears and laughter, and children in perpetual motion. We spilled out into the yard, the street, the beach—especially the beach, the center of our days.

The routine was easy. We awoke, took our turns in the bathroom, pulled on our shorts and tops, and ate breakfast under mothers' watchful eyes. We rolled bathing suits into our towels, tucked them under our arms, and strolled out together for the fourteen-block walk, a herd of carefree kids. Somewhere in our midst was an aunt or two to shepherd the flock. Mother would arrive around noon with our lunch. We had soft white bread sandwiches, gritty from the sand on our fingers, filled with cheese or bologna or peanut butter and jelly. Carrot sticks, slabs of watermelon, and thermos bottles of milk were added to the menu. I hated the milk, but even worse than the milk was the one-hour-after-meal wait until we could escape back into the water.

When the hour was up, we raced each other back into the ocean, splashing, kicking, jumping foam-crested waves, backs turned against the impact as they crashed over us. We plunged forward, flopping on our bellies to swim out beyond Mother and the aunts, who stood mid-calf in the water, gripping the seaweed-covered side ropes of the approved swimming area. They shrieked with glee when unexpected waves rolled in higher and stronger than anticipated, splashing cold salty water over their bodies.

We swam out to the far cross-rope where no aunt would dare to go, where the water was deep and the tide could still pull. We sat on the rope, traded stories and dares, swam and floated, and rode the waves in to shore on our stomachs.

When called in by Mother or an aunt who thought we'd been in the water too long, we built sandcastles, searched the beach for interesting seashells, or dug deep holes in an attempt to reach China. Too often, someone, usually my older brother Allan, suggested climbing the rocks of the jetty. It frightened me to jump between the slippery ocean-wet rocks where they stretched into the sea, but for fear of being called a scaredy-cat, I would never let the others know. It was a relief when the hot summer sun and our own activity sent us dashing back into the water.

As a child, I never thought of those annual summer gatherings as family reunions—I probably didn't even know the words. I thought of them as magical days, when cousins morphed into extra brothers and another sister, and aunts became extra mothers who settled disputes, stuck a Band-Aid on scrapes, dispensed sympathy, and handed out treats.

It was during those summers that I learned to share, and it was then I learned what family bonds were all about. Back then, I thought of those summers as magical days, and I still do today.ᕱ

Dinner at Dora's

by Margaret A. Frey | *Delanco, New Jersey*

FROM MY EARLIEST MEMORY until the year I turned twenty-one, Thanksgiving dinner was held at Dora's farm in Delanco, New Jersey. Dora wasn't a relative, but I knew she and my grandmother, Franny, both widowed, had grown up together along the Jersey shore. Dora cooked and served the meal, but she never shared it with us. Franny paid for the feast in advance. I never saw Dora beyond the holiday or considered the arrangement odd or unusual. It was simply the way our family, the Prices, celebrated the holiday. The summer ended, school started, leaves fell off the trees, and it was time for dinner at Dora's.

Dora was a tall, broad woman, but I never thought her fat. She was solid the way the river wall was solid, holding the water in check, sure and fast. She wore her hair in a lopsided bun with renegade strands flying loose around a coarse, florid face. If Dora had a last name, I never heard it. For my eight cousins, my sister, and me, she was the Turkey Lady, who greeted us with a harried wave and "Happy Holiday," always dressed in the same outfit: white blouse, long black skirt, and brown leather apron.

Dora's farmhouse, tucked off the main road, sat plain and squat behind a stand of leafless oak and maple trees. The clapboard house dated back to the early 1900s with ancient gas fixtures and no central heat. Off the front of the house were holding pens for chickens, goats, and squealing pigs. An exotic, long-necked creature in a back pen watched while we tumbled from our cars into the ragged yard. My sister, Kat, called the thick-lashed animal Lamb Chop because she loved the puppeteer, Shari Lewis. The creature turned out to be a Bolivian llama, named Tonto.

My mother winced at the dusty barnyard and again at the state of the house. Dogs raced from the threshold, barking and thumping bushy tails, and overfed cats threaded through legs with noisy greetings. Mother sniffed and said the place needed a good scrubbing.

With the exception of the dining room, the rooms of the farmhouse were tiny and dark. The parlor's main feature, a potbellied stove, steamed up the windows with a blasting heat, and boisterous children discovered early on how the stove could sizzle the skin off of a careless hand or elbow. Cautiously, we navigated the cast-iron monster then raced and bumped up the narrow staircase, dragging our woolen coats and scarves. Halfway up the stairs, the air turned thin and frigid, and our breath streamed white between slaps and giggles. We raced down the hallway to the back bedrooms where we jumped and wrestled on the squeaky, spring-coiled beds. It was a wild tour of a living museum without the finger-wagging guards to spoil the fun.

Dora rang a brass bell when dinner was ready. The bell was not like the dainty one my mother used, but rather a hardy captain's bell. Once it rang, we stumbled down the staircase, stood in wriggling formation for hair inspections, shirt tucks, and hankie-spit cleanups, and then marched into the dining room where rowdy behavior came to an end. A long table covered in bleached linen featured crystal, silver cutlery, and white bone china. Brightly lit, the room glistened and shined. Dora, though rough around the edges, stunned us into civilized behavior. She knew the power of presentation. It worked every time.

In the late fifties and early sixties, there were eighteen Prices at the table: ten wormy children and eight adults. Franny, the undisputed matriarch, took her place at the head of the table. Like Dora, she was a large, imposing woman. In a steady voice, she spoke about the year's passing, the family's health and good fortune, and then led us in a moment of prayer. With a quick "Amen," she signaled Dora and the traditional, belt-straining meal began.

Only once was the dinner ruined, when my cousin, Roger, smirked and said the turkey stuffing was Dora's special sweetbread concoction, laced with llama innards. Kat dropped her fork immediately. My father tried to laugh it off, but it was too late. We secretly fed our portion to the dogs.

Like all children, we grew older and less rambunctious. Dora's house sadly lost its mystery and charm. I spotted cobwebs in the corners and mouse droppings on the floor. Old rivalries and squabbles between my father and his younger brothers brewed and swelled, but the dinners remained a constant in our lives until Franny passed on in 1975.

Following Franny's death, Dora called to offer condolences. I discovered then that she and my grandmother had both left school in the sixth grade to take work at a textile factory. One morning Franny had been overcome by the heat and exhaustion and nearly tipped backward into a vat of lye. Dora managed to reach out and break her fall.

"That was a thousand years ago," Dora said, with a deep-throated laugh. "Your grandmother was a generous woman. Those holiday dinners caught on until I was turning people away. Had myself a nice little business, all right. It kept me going through the hard winters.

Your grandmother saw me through the lean times. God'll bless her for that."

I wonder now if the holiday wasn't Franny's sly invention, an orchestrated family tradition that happened to catch on. Her signature remains indelibly stamped on my own holiday dinners, a day when adult spats are temporarily suspended, and petty complaints and resentments curbed and parked outside the door.

I recall the earlier model every autumn, those years when we were young and strong, bursting with dreams and antsy vitality. It was when we were the Price family and Thanksgiving was more than a meal. It meant sharing Franny's unique vision of family, fellowship, and enduring gratitude through an act of communion, the breaking of bread. It meant dinner at Dora's.

God bless them both for that. ❧

A Southern Family Reunion

by Sandy Williams Driver | *Albertville, Alabama*

THE MORROW'S FAMILY REUNION ISN'T ANYTHING FANCY. It's always been about family, down-home cooking, and bluegrass music . . . in that order. Like many other Southern families in Alabama, we place a heap of importance on our kinfolks, and the pleasure of good food is at the heart of all our get-togethers.

Eight years after the death of R. C. Morrow, his twelve children gathered together with their spouses, children, grandchildren, and great-grandchildren in Albertville, Alabama, the hometown of their ancestors. The family spent the breezy May afternoon in the beautiful Southern outdoors eating, playing music, and remembering the great man who started their large clan back in the early 1900s.

R. C. Morrow was a big man with a twinkle in his watery blue eyes and a banjo on his strong knee. He taught his children the importance of family and good music while his wife, Dollie, kept their brood close to home with her delicious cooking and gentle heart.

It was evident at our first-ever reunion that the sons and daughters were intent on keeping the traditions of their parents alive. Good fellowship, mouthwatering food, and lively music filled the afternoon event. On that day, 156 heads were counted in the local park, where an enormous outdoor pavilion provided welcome shade from the brilliant sunlight.

A broad range of ages was represented at the reunion, from the newest great-great-grandchild, born just three weeks prior, to the oldest surviving member, Uncle Juddy, who had recently celebrated his eightieth birthday. Most of the family still lived within easy driving distance of Albertville, high atop beautiful Sand Mountain, but a few stray kinfolk, from as far away as Michigan and California, answered the call to come home for a day of togetherness and reminiscing.

The cool cement floor of the gathering spot was loaded with plenty of comfortable lawn chairs, and long folding tables straining under the weight of oval serving platters and deep glass bowls. The specialties of the day were crispy fried chicken, fluffy mashed potatoes, spicy cornbread dressing, salty pinto beans, smooth creamed-style corn, golden buttery biscuits, and thick slices of juicy, red tomatoes picked earlier that morning from nearby family gardens.

The dessert tables were a popular hangout, especially for the men in the family who quickly forgot their doctor's warnings for just one day. My aunts brought their famous biscuit puddings and legendary strawberry pies. The banana pudding bowls on the heavily laden table were the first ones emptied, then the peach cobbler pies vanished—a close second. Before long, friendly rivalries sprang up over which one was better: Aunt Ilene's pecan pie or Aunt Barbara's coconut cake. I never could decide myself.

After everyone had their fill, the few remaining leftovers were quickly placed in coolers to keep uninvited bugs away. The men patted their bulging stomachs and settled down to exchange tall-tales of oversized catfish, and to watch the little ones play on the adjoining playground. The women huddled together in small groups, swapping old family recipes and sipping mouth-puckeringly sweet tea from clear plastic cups.

It wasn't long before Uncle Juke's son, Hoyt, slipped away to retrieve his shiny guitar from the trunk of his car. Another cousin, Robby, suddenly remembered he had placed an old banjo behind his truck seat, just in case anyone wanted him to pick a song or two.

When the two joined together and began their rendition of Grandpa's favorite tune, "Bile Dem Cabbage Down," voices hushed to a whisper and chairs were scooted closer to the delightful entertainment. Even the children abandoned their fascination with the jungle gym for the sounds of the sweet bluegrass music, which ran through their veins and filled their souls with warmth.

Uncle Harvey and Uncle Raymond jumped to their feet and amused everyone with their buck-dancing expertise, despite the exasperated looks from their wives. Foot-stomping and hand-clapping music like "Wabash Cannonball" and "Dueling Banjos" drifted through the honeysuckle scented air and brought smiles to the glowing faces bearing a striking similarity to the man who will never be forgotten.

Morrows, old and young alike, ended that memorable day with a song in their hearts, a twinkle in their eyes, and a full stomach. Grandpa would have been proud.

Perfect Pitch

by Lanita Bradley Boyd | *Hendersonville, Tennessee*

I COME FROM A FAMILY OF SINGERS. When my father was young, he played in a local country band and discovered that he had a knack for playing a multitude of instruments. As I grew up, and for many years afterward, Mother and Daddy hosted "musicals" in our home. Daddy played the fiddle, guitar, piano, and organ. As a special treat, he played his saw, using his fiddle bow on it to produce lonely, wailing tunes.

Friends and neighbors got together purely for the love of music. They played everything from gospel to bluegrass to pop, the singing usually some form of gospel. Daddy was also a great a cappella singer, who used an "A" tuning fork to obtain the correct pitch. Together, as a family, we sang lively Christian music before it became the popular thing to do.

The first family get-together after my father died was naturally a very sad time for the family. We had no spirit for singing. Daddy had been the organizer and motivator of our songfests. Finally, we agreed that we had to sing a few songs, if only to honor his memory.

We all gathered in the living room and my brother, John, looked around the room.

"Give us an A, Larry," he said. But before Larry could produce his tuning fork and strike it against his book, we all froze at the ringing sound that filled the room. As the ringing began to subside, Larry pulled out his own tuning fork and stuck it. The pitch matched perfectly.

We had no idea where the mysterious pitch had come from, and it has never happened again. Was Daddy's spirit still there with us? We felt so.

A scientist who loved to tinker, Daddy had enjoyed our family's singing sessions so much that he'd made a habit of keeping a cassette recorder around. And though each of us had some form of aged tape in our possession, it had been a long time since anything new had been recorded. Recently, we all gathered in the living room again and sang together again.

"We sound pretty good," John said. "We ought to tape our singing like Daddy used to do."

"I think we should make a CD!" his thirteen-year-old daughter, Katie, volunteered. "You know, our neighbors run a recording studio. Maybe they'd let us record there. We could do it when we're all together again." We all chuckled, pleased with the idea.

After various e-mails and phone calls—from Tennessee and California and Kentucky and Indiana, between brothers and sister, and niece and aunts and uncles—the arrangements were made. We had a sumptuous feast and opened a multitude of gifts, then headed for the nearby city of Hendersonville, Tennessee, a Nashville suburb. There, we were greeted warmly by Liliana Kohann and Voytek Kochanekn, Polish immigrants who operated the recording studio. We were impressed by the autographed pictures on their walls and the elaborate recording set-up.

Katie, who had compiled a list of songs from the requests of various group members, told us which songs we'd be singing from the three different hymnals she'd brought along. Before we began,

Voytek suggested we sing straight through with only a slight pause between songs.

Once we got started, Liliana was very impressed with the quality of our singing.

"Such wonderful harmonies," she exclaimed as she moved among us, snapping pictures as she spoke. When we took a break between the Christian music and the carols, she asked, "Did you practice a lot for this?"

"Not any," Mother answered.

"Not today," I added. "But we've been singing together for forty years."

But despite Liliana's praise, there were times during that session when I had a little trouble with my voice. As I looked around at the group—my dad's ninety-one-year-old sister, my eighty-year-old mother, my two brothers and their spouses, their children and their spouses, and one great-grandchild, Kinley—my eyes welled up and my throat constricted. Surely this was a taste of heaven itself.

Then Gina picked up her daughter, Kinley. "Would you like to sing a song?" she asked. At two-and-a-half years of age, Kinley, who has her great-grandfather's knack for being on pitch, was quite the accomplished singer. With no preliminaries, Kinley started singing "Jesus Loves Me." Immediately, I understood Voytek's wisdom in recording straight through without stopping. As Gina moved Kinley closer to the microphone, we all hummed or sang softly in the background. Kinley sang the entire verse and chorus, ending with a strong "the Bible tells me so-o-o." After the briefest moment of silence, we broke into spontaneous applause. A new generation was taking up the tradition.

Daddy sometimes had a Scrooge attitude about the holidays, but he loved to take a group caroling. During the holidays, he always made sure we visited all the homes of the elderly and shut-ins in the community. And at the end of each session, Daddy had a particular concluding routine, so on this day as we finished the last of the carols, we looked toward Josh, the youngest taught by Daddy. Josh understood. He raised his fingers, silently signaling 1-2-3. Then together we shouted, "Merry Christmas!"

Though it was our twentieth Christmas without Daddy, there was no doubt in our minds that his influence and spirit would be with us today and for generations to come.

The Town of
Hendersonville, Tennessee

Population: 42,216

Town Facts

First incorporated • Hendersonville was incorporated in 1968, following an election to incorporate an area of approximately 0.2 square miles. The new town commenced operation on July 26, 1969, and one night in 1972, the city commission annexed a vast area surrounding the 0.2 square mile. Overnight, the population of Hendersonville rose from about 400 to 17,000.

Origin of the name • Hendersonville was named after Colonel William Henderson, a Revolutionary War veteran who was named the first postmaster of Hendersonville, Tennessee, by an act of Congress in 1800.

Transportation and Industry • For many years, Hendersonville was an important stop on the Louisville and Nashville L&N Railroad, with a depot for passenger service from 1859 until 1933. The only break in service was a period during the Civil War when the Union forces took control of the railroad. From 1913 until 1932, the Interurban Railway—an electric train—operated between Hendersonville and Nashville. Today, there is no passenger train service available in Hendersonville. Transportation is available by boat. The town's largest industries today are Aladdin Temp-Rite, which produces insulated food service systems, and MGM Window Company, which manufactures insulated glass.

Location • The town of Hendersonville is located on the northeastern border of Nashville, Tennessee, on the banks of the Cumberland River and Old Hickory Lake, approximately 25 miles south of the Kentucky border.

Interesting Facts

Known as the "City on the Lake," Hendersonville has 26 miles of shoreline. Old Hickory Lake is named after President Andrew Jackson, whose nickname was Old Hickory because he was said to "stand tall in battle like an old hickory tree." ❧

The Bradleys of Hendersonville

When Lanita Bradley Boyd was a preschooler, her Aunt Deba and Aunt Mina, students at Hendersonville High, taught her to shout, "Yay, rah, Hendersonville!" on every sports occasion—even at Portland games when Hendersonville was not playing. Now her brother John Bradley lives there and is the Hendersonville city attorney, and his daughter Katie (Mary Katherine Bradley) attends Hendersonville High School. ❧

Interesting People

One of the first settlers in the area was Daniel Smith. Smith, an officer in the Revolutionary War, was commissioned by the State of North Carolina to survey the North Carolina/Kentucky state line. Smith mapped the area now known as Middle Tennessee. He loved the area so much that he stayed. His house, Rock Castle, built in 1784, still stands near the center of town. Smith served as chairman of the committee to adopt a constitution for Tennessee, which gained statehood in 1796, and later served as a United States senator and Indian treaty negotiator.

Hendersonville's close proximity to Nashville made it a haven for country music stars and other recording artists. Famous names who called Hendersonville home include Johnny Cash, June Carter Cash, Roy Orbison, Conway Twitty, Roy Acuff, Barbara Mandrell, Leon Russell, Merle Haggard, Ricky Skaggs, Dan Seals, Tammy Wynette, George Jones, and the Oak Ridge Boys. ❧

Wilbur's Vanishing Act

by Michelle Close Mills | *Butler, Indiana*

WHEN I WAS TEN YEARS OLD, around 1915, our family sold our farm on the Indiana/Ohio state line and moved a short distance to the small town of Butler, Indiana. Dad opened a grocery store and bought our family a big home just up the street.

Our home was a happy place that seemed to attract children, which was no problem with my folks. Dad adored kids, and he was happiest when surrounded by a bunch of them. We threw a lot of parties over the years, but when I was a senior in high school, Mom and Dad held an unforgettable costume gala for my friends and me. We scheduled it for the Saturday night before Halloween. My date for the party was my boyfriend, Horace, whom I had met while visiting family in nearby Edgerton, Ohio. He was the same age as me, and a musician with the band that was playing for a dance at my cousin Vera's school. I will never forget the day we met. It was the same night President Warren Harding died.

Horace, considered quite a catch, lived in Montpelier, Ohio, where his father was a doctor. He was a good-looking boy, with blonde hair, sparkling green eyes, and a great sense of humor. But the thing that made Horace most appealing to me was his car, or rather his father's car.

Because of the considerable distance between our two homes, it was necessary to have reliable transportation, and Horace's father had that base covered. The doctor didn't drive just any old car, either. He owned a beautiful, hunter-green 1921 Cadillac, which he'd christened with the name Wilbur. Because Horace was allowed to drive Wilbur to and from our dates, it wasn't long before I was the envy of every female in Butler under the age of twenty-five. I felt like a queen as Horace and I sailed around town, listening to the engine purr, all the while pitying "the little people" who weren't lucky enough to have a luxurious car to drive. I loved Wilbur!

Since we had had a problem with pranksters at our last party, Horace expressed concerns about where to park Wilbur to avoid any mischief from uninvited guests. Dad told him to lock everything up and park the car alongside the house. He assured Horace that between the two of them, Wilbur would be well guarded.

The hours ticked by as the party cranked into high gear. At about nine o'clock, Horace left me beside the punch bowl with Vera while he went outside to check on the car. A few moments later, an ear-splitting howl of anguish brought the party to a halt. Vera was so startled that she spewed a large mouthful of red punch, narrowly missing the fluffy carnation-pink skirt of my Little Bo Peep costume.

Dad and I immediately ran out through the pantry door, followed by an armada of spooks, witches, fairytale characters, a mailbox, a knight in shining armor, and several assorted woodland animals.

Horace was hunched over, clutching his chest, gasping for air.

"Young man, what is the meaning of such a racket?" Dad bellowed.

"Breathe, Horace, breathe!" I shouted. "Tell us what's wrong!"

"Somebody has taken Wilbur!"

"Who on earth is Wilbur?" inquired the Fairy Godmother.

"Isn't Wilbur the new kid at school?" asked the Knight. "For heaven sakes why would anyone want to take him?"

"Maybe Wilbur is another one of Helen's cousins," offered the Mailbox.

"Certainly not," retorted Vera, who was masquerading as Little Red Riding Hood.

"Oh, no," I moaned, realizing that Wilbur's disappearance was a very bad thing, indeed.

After everyone was briefed as to Wilbur's true identity, Dad and my older brother, Lloyd, organized a search party. Our curious band of would-be trick-or-treaters split up into small groups to find the missing Cadillac. I tagged along with Dad, Lloyd, and Horace.

"If anyone has laid one scratch on Wilbur, they'll be sorry!" Horace fumed as he stomped along.

"I'll thank you to keep a civil tongue in your head and continue looking for the blasted car," Dad snapped, still miffed by the disruption to our carefully planned evening.

We found Wilbur a few blocks away, behind an old barn, camouflaged by a mound of hay. Horace was so relieved that he seemed ready to cry. But his relief soon dissolved into disgust, as he began to remove the mess from the car.

"Who would want to do such a thing to you, Wilbur?" he lamented.

"Probably someone that didn't like you and my daughter sashaying around in that fancy rig when they were forced to walk," Dad responded, his good humor restored.

"I'm not taking any more chances," Horace declared. "Once the car is cleaned up, I'm going home."

Horace was true to his word.

When he drove out of sight that evening, it was the last time that I ever saw him. I guess one minor brush with the mysterious car vandal was enough to convince him that he needed to find a girlfriend closer to home. Sadly I realized that when Horace left, the much beloved Wilbur left with him, signaling an end to our luxurious dates.

But when I think of it now, I'm sure it was for the best. If Horace had ever proposed marriage, I would have eventually wondered whom I was marrying: Horace or Wilbur?

Unfailing Love

by Rita Chandler | *Morrilton, Arkansas*

"WHY ISN'T JIM HERE YET?" Daddy asked and then checked the clock once more before searching the driveway for his eldest son's car. "Thought maybe he'd be one of the first to arrive."

My parents had planned their sixtieth wedding anniversary celebration, expecting all four of their children to attend. In spite of the debilitating pain in one of Daddy's legs, he and Mama had looked forward to the event.

The big question on everyone's mind was Jim. Would my oldest brother, who lived nearby, come to the party with his wife and daughter? Several years before, an innocent conversation had erupted into a full-blown quarrel between Jim and my sister, Jane. Since then, they had avoided one another, even for family gatherings.

My father had spent his life farming the unyielding soil near Morrilton, in central Arkansas. He wrestled the land to produce food for his family and provide a cash crop that covered the bare essentials.

Uneducated and fatherless since the age of sixteen, he seldom complained about the hard years of long toil with no luxuries. My mother, Hazel, the girl he married when he was just twenty-one, stayed by his side throughout the Depression years, drought, and flood, sharing equally in the work and in the rewards of watching the children mature and establish their own families.

My youngest brother lived just down the road and now owned the family farm. He and his wife and their two daughters had arranged the party. My sister, Jane, and her husband planned to arrive early, driving from North Little Rock. Of the four children, I was the one who lived farthest away, in California. Absent from the fiftieth anniversary festivities because of major surgery, I had firmly resolved to attend the celebration of their sixtieth.

For this milestone, Daddy replaced his worn overalls and patched shirt with a Sunday shirt, colorful tie, and dress pants. He sat in his big chair, his chrome-plated walker nearby, his eyes facing the windows toward the front driveway.

He loved the land my grandparents had bought before Mama's birth and had purchased the same farm after fourteen years of share-cropping. The familiar landscape revived many happy memories, but on this day, his eyes scanned the driveway for Jim's car only.

Lifelong friends arrived, many with children and grandchildren. An assortment of aunts, uncles, cousins, and other relatives and friends congregated. Guests greeted and embraced the honored couple and one another. Babies passed from one person's arms to the next. Small children dressed in holiday finery garnered hugs and loving pats as they raced around the house, clutching toys.

Mama, radiant in a blue dress, her white hair combed in an attractive upsweep, enjoyed her position of recognition. She spoke to each person, thanking him or her for coming and for helping make the day more special.

As cars entered the driveway, Daddy's old eyes searched for his firstborn. He addressed his friends with pleasure, but as the next car approached, he stretched to identify the newest arrivals. I hovered near my father, concerned for him as he voiced his sadness.

"Do you think Jim will come?" he asked my husband Ben, as he wiped tears with the back of his hand. "Never done anythin' agin' him. Loaned him money for his first house. Helped him more than once. Didn't give us no trouble growin' up."

"Nothing you've done." Ben replied. "I'm sure he's not angry with you."

"You're right. He's mad at his sister. Think Jim would be here if he hadn't quarreled with Jane?" His voice trembled as he blew his nose.

Daddy seldom expressed his deep feelings, but Ben's relationship as son-in-law allowed him to confide.

I tried erasing the painful scene of my father looking for my brother, but as the hours ticked by, Daddy kept checking the window, asking the same question that no one could answer. His small, withered body seemed to shrink, his watery eyes sad.

Daddy slowly shook his head. "He's not coming. I'm old and not worth much anymore. He needed to be here. Might not get another chance."

As a youngster, I had rushed to my parents for comfort. Now our roles were reversed. I wanted to heal the hurt and the breach—an impossible task. The consequences of the quarrel between my siblings caused an ever-widening circle, creating unforeseen pain.

With deep longing, I took one more glance out the window and caught a glimpse of my brother's car being parked underneath the oak trees. It was easy to identify his white Cadillac in the midst of beat-up farm trucks and modest sedans.

As Jim and his family walked unhurriedly into the house, Daddy's face lit up, his body revitalizing right before my eyes like a wilted plant freshly watered. He stood up, reaching out both arms to enfold my brother's shoulders. Hugs and smiles dissolved the pain of Jim's late arrival. No one asked about the delay nor sought an explanation.

I wanted to shout at my brother and sister, "Do you realize the pain you've caused?" But I knew I must not. My parents would react as they had in the past when my siblings or I caused them anguish—they welcomed and forgave without confrontation. If our family had followed Daddy and Mama's example, there never would be any broken ties.

"Jim, I'm so glad to see you!" Daddy's voice carried to the furthest corners of the house. Then his eyes sought those of my mother, his smile beaming with pride. "Hazel! Look who's here!"

The Windswept Prairie

by Roberta Rhodes | *Cheyenne, Wyoming*

Over the river and through the woods,
To Grandmother's house we go!

ISN'T THAT WHAT WE ALWAYS THINK OF at Thanksgiving, no matter where Grandmother lives? Whether the rivers and trees are of the natural variety or whether the rivers are traffic amid towering timber-like buildings, all roads lead to Grandmother's at Thanksgiving.

But with my grandmother, the journey meant neither trees nor traffic. Her house clung tenaciously to a piece of windswept prairie, near one end of a 320-acre plot in Wyoming, populated by nothing but greasewood, jackrabbits, and coyotes. The rivers we crossed were only dry gulches, and there were no woods.

In 1910, Grandpa, an Iowan lured by the promise of land, moved his family to Wyoming, lock, stock, and barrel. To build a house, he had to cut timber in the mountains, some 20 miles to the west, and haul it down by team and wagon. The house—two rooms and a sleeping loft—may have been "pioneer-purty," but by the time I came along it had turned gray, the color of ancient, weathered wood, and the porch was a hopscotch of splintering boards. But during the late 1930s and early 1940s it was *the* family gathering place on Thanksgiving.

I can't tell you that the aroma of roasting turkey filled those two rooms because, frankly, I don't remember. I do remember an abundance of food. And I remember the aunts each hovering in a proprietary manner over their own particular pies. But mostly, I remember after-dinner events.

The children scurried out to play, the men disappeared, and the women went to the kitchen to "do dishes."

To be admitted into the kitchen to do dishes with the women was a rite of passage. Little girls were shooed out. The kitchen was the place for woman-talk, deemed inappropriate for innocent little ears. In the kitchen, women talked about who was getting married, who was having a baby, and the most curious talk of all, who was suffering from that mysterious, indefinable malady known as "female trouble." The conversations were good-natured, gossipy, and fun, and all took place under the guise of "doing dishes." Once a girl had been admitted into the kitchen, she was regarded as a woman among women. As a preteen, I was one of the barred innocents. But my turn would come.

Each Thanksgiving, my uncles, who had been boasting all year about who had the better car, had set out to prove their claim on the big hill just north of the house.

"Come on, you cowards," a man's voice called. "Let's settle this now."

On these high plains there were no shrubs, no trees. There were no neighbors to be considered. The only obstacles were the coarse, rocky surface and gravity. The uncles would put their cars in gear, rev up the engines, then chug and grunt their way to the top of the hill, backwards. I don't recall anyone's car ever making it all the way to the top, but bragging rights—until the next year—definitely belonged to the one who made it the farthest.

After that, everyone migrated back to the house amid playful jostling and laughter. Once settled inside, the family listened to Grandpa and Grandma's stories of the early days, from 1910 to 1915. Mostly, they spoke of the isolation. Grandpa worked in the mountains all week—home on Sunday and then back to work on Monday. The nearest neighbors, homesteaders themselves, were several miles away across the wind-woven prairies. Food was transported once a month on horseback or by wagon from Cheyenne, a bustling cow town of about 11,000 people.

We loved hearing about the day Grandma, alone as usual with her three small children, saw several Native Americans on horseback stop at the well a few yards from the kitchen door. Stories of trouble persisted, even at that late date, and Grandma was taking no chances. She sent her children scurrying up to the sleeping loft to hide under the bed, in those days just a straw-filled tick on a plank frame, while she grabbed the shotgun and headed for the porch. She sat there—the gun across her lap—as the Native Americans watered their horses, then rode peacefully away.

Someone also recalled the big blizzard of 1912. It brought twenty-four inches of snow to the prairie and marooned the family for weeks. The relentless wind packed snow into gullies and howled around the corners of the house. Supplies were low. Fort Russell was 10 miles away, Cheyenne 14 miles. Town was impossible to reach, even if the snow stopped falling, which it didn't.

When the firewood ran out, Grandpa cut the tops off the fence posts and used them for fuel. But when the food ran out, Grandpa knew they were in trouble.

"Unless the Lord sends it, we'll have no breakfast tomorrow," he said.

Early the next morning, the entire family was awakened by a hollow-sounding *ka-thump* just outside the house. A wild pigeon, rare in those parts, had flown into the wire of their makeshift telephone and fallen to the ground. Breakfast had arrived!

At the mention of food, we were jogged back to the present.

Reluctantly, mothers and aunts began collecting their dishes and pie pans. It had been a great day, but it was time to go.

We said our goodbyes and started our trek "over the prairies and through the wind" to our homes in Cheyenne, each cherishing the memories that wrapped us in love and reminded us that we belonged somewhere, that we had family. And that together we could brave anything.⌒

A Jaunt to Aunt Josie's

by Mary Ralph Bradley | *Ralph Hollow, Tennessee*

THE FOURTH OF NINE CHILDREN, I was born in the house my carpenter father built in 1919, on a hilly Tennessee farm called Vertical Plains. My parents wanted us to experience life beyond the holler we lived in—where you could see the sun only by looking straight up—so Daddy, a self-educated man, usually took us into Nashville for special occasions. We made the fifteen-mile trip into town for the state fair, the circus, and even once to see President Roosevelt when he drove through town.

But on one special Sunday every year, all eleven of us piled into my father's old 1929 Pontiac to make a bigger journey—a round trip of 120 miles. The crowd wasn't complete, however, until we'd picked up Grandmammy Martin, because we were going to see her sister, Aunt Josie.

"Now, every one of you has to behave yourselves," Mama reminded as soon as Grandmammy came out the front door wearing a pretty calico dress covered by a snowy white apron.

With a little juggling, now twelve of us settled into that old blue car. Mama and Daddy sat in the front with the three littlest,

Mina, Deba, and Wallace. The rest of us fit into the back seat, neatly arranged. There was never a doubt about how to sit. We'd done this before. One of us sat up, one sat back, one sat up, one sat back, one sat up, and the last one sat back. Grandmammy always sat back, ready to tap any one of us on the head at the least sign of misbehavior.

And as the trip commenced, no matter how much fun we children had, Grandmammy had more. She laughed and joked and told us stories along the way.

Our version of fun was to tease each other as we rambled down the dusty road.

"There's Evelyn's house!" I would cry as we passed a ramshackle house.

To get even, Evelyn would yell, "Then that shed out back is your house!"

"Look!" L.D. hollered, seeing two ragamuffins by the roadside. "There's Jimmy T. and his big brother!" Then everyone squealed with glee. L.D., the most mischievous one in the family, had accidentally insulted himself as well as Jimmy T. It was always fun to get something on our big brother.

Carleen and Juanita, the two eldest, disdained our foolishness, but even they could not help laughing now and then. The rough miles slowly passed—Hendersonville, Murfreesboro, Woodbury, McMinnville, and on to Viola. Mama and Daddy spoke in low tones up front, paying no attention to us, assured that we were well behaved right behind them.

After about four hours, we arrived at Aunt Josie's long, rambling farmhouse with its welcoming front porch. She and Uncle Rube lived near railroad tracks, but otherwise were far removed from civilization. As soon as the car stopped, we poured out. Some of us ran inside to visit the relatives. Some of us ran to visit the outhouse.

Uncle Rube, with his long white whiskers and mustache, welcomed us with dancing eyes and a big hug. Aunt Josie, a bit chunkier and grayer than her younger sister, hugged Grandmammy.

"Catherine," she said, "you're a sight for sore eyes. I was so tickled when I got Hester's letter that ya'll were coming up." Then she hugged Mama, and each of us in turn. Looking at the baby she was seeing for the first time, she smiled at Mama. "He's the prettiest one you've ever had."

We busied ourselves all afternoon on the tire swing and exploring the big yard and the woods nearby. Then my brothers led the way to the railroad tracks and we younger ones followed.

Aunt Josie held baby Wallace for a few minutes before handing him to Daddy so she could help Grandmammy and Mama finish up in the kitchen. Known to the world as Luther D. Ralph, Daddy didn't mind. He was a man before his time. Daddy was known in our community for having a baby in his arms, a bottle in his pocket, and one or two small ones clinging to his legs.

Soon, Sunday dinner was announced with the clanging of the dinner bell. We came running. It was time to put on our Sunday manners. Everyone remembered his or her "Yes, ma'am" and "No, ma'am" and "Yes, please," and "No, thank you," to keep from embarrassing Mama and Daddy.

Aunt Josie's big family was grown and gone, so her bountiful table was long enough for all of us. No one there had to "take an old cold tater and wait," as we'd often heard sung on the *Grand Ole Opry*. Big slices of country ham from Uncle Rube's smokehouse, golden-brown fried chicken, green beans, fried corn, fried okra, and fried apples, squash (which most didn't eat), sliced tomatoes, mashed potatoes, turnip greens, sweet potatoes, fluffy white biscuits, and tall glasses of spring-cooled milk from their own cows was spread before us.

This once-a-year treat was almost more than our eyes, let alone our stomachs, could stand. Mama was a good cook, but nobody could compete with Aunt Josie.

My dad, the jokester, couldn't resist asking, "Aunt Josie, couldn't you think of something else to cook?" Aunt Josie laughed along. She would have been disappointed if he hadn't teased her in some way.

After the main meal came dessert: chocolate pie, chocolate cake, and cherry pie. Aunt Josie enjoyed watching us eat and urged everyone to have a second piece. L.D. did, but Daddy was more interested in Uncle Rube's sorghum molasses, which was always on hand from the sorghum mill nearby. As soon as it was passed to his end of the table, he poured the thick brown molasses onto his plate. Using his knife, he scooped it up over his biscuit. Seeing how much Daddy enjoyed that dark, rich delicacy, Uncle Rube always gave him a bucketful to take home.

In those days, company never overstayed their welcome. Even though it was a long trip, we never lingered much longer than dinner and dessert. And as soon as Daddy stood up, even before he spoke, we knew the fun was over.

"All right, children," he said, "It's time to go."

We knew better than to argue. We knew we had to get home before dark. We had cows, hogs, and chickens at home needing our attention.

Through the years, I've had many enjoyable trips to visit relatives. I've gone from Nashville to Washington, D.C., Oklahoma, New York, and California, but oftentimes my mind wanders back to another place, a special place called Vertical Plains. Nothing has ever surpassed or dimmed the memory of our annual jaunts to see Aunt Josie and Uncle Rube, and nothing ever will.◡

The Best Present

by Lynn R. Hartz | *Charleston, West Virginia*

I KNEW I WOULD NOT BE ABLE to go to my grandparent's fiftieth wedding anniversary. I also knew that I would be the only family member not in attendance. But it just could not be helped.

My grandparents had not been young people when they married. In the thinking of 1919, the year they married, my grandmother was probably considered an old maid. Today, we would call her a career woman. She taught school for twelve years, earning her first-class teaching certificate as well as a principal's certification before marrying my grandfather. Granddaddy was a railroad man. He met my grandmother when she was taking some students on a train ride to an amusement park. Interestingly, the house that they bought was built exactly where the streets of the amusement park had been a few years earlier.

They had five daughters. I was the eldest granddaughter and was named after my grandmother. Although her name was Malinda, she was always called Lynn. Whenever I answered her telephone, it seemed strange to me to hear the caller ask for Lynn. She was Grandma to me!

I really wanted to be with my grandparents for their anniversary party. It had been a long time since I'd seen them. Because they were older, we'd had a fortieth anniversary party for them, too. Life is sometimes too short, and we might have missed a time for joy had we waited. But now it was time for the bigger celebration, and I wouldn't be able to attend. Everyone would be there—aunts, uncles, cousins, great-aunts, and all the people from the other side of my family, too, as well as the people from the churches they attended. I would miss the best social gathering of the year, but there was absolutely nothing that I could do to change things. It was a 200-mile drive, my husband was in the air force, and I was expecting my first child—any day.

On the Friday before the party, I went to the doctor for a check-up and asked, "Do you think it might be possible that this baby could arrive tomorrow?"

"Well, it could," he said. "We could help it along a little. Why do you want it tomorrow?"

I told him that it was my grandparents' fiftieth wedding anniversary and that since I couldn't be there, I thought it would be really nice if we could gift them with a grandchild on their special day.

The doctor thought it was a nice idea, too, and we made plans to meet at the hospital early the next morning. I guess we all had the same idea, including the baby, because by the time we both arrived at the hospital, I was already dilated and my water had broken. But even with an intravenous drip, labor seemed to take forever. Finally, at ten minutes after four in the afternoon, our precious baby girl was born. She had arrived in time.

I could hardly wait to telephone my grandparents. We hadn't yet told anyone that I had been admitted to the hospital, and I wanted them to be the first to know.

Calling long distance from a hospital telephone took a little maneuvering. There was a three-hour difference on the east coast, so it would be just after 7 P.M. at my grandparents' home, and the still be going strong. We finally managed to have the ∼ges billed to our home phone and placed the call. When I heard Grandma's voice on the other end, I was overcome with emotion.

"Hello? Grandma? You have a beautiful granddaughter!" I was so excited, I could barely speak, my voice breaking as tears of exhaustion and homesickness combined and flowed down my cheeks.

"Oh, Granddaughter!" she exclaimed. "Oh! How did you do this?" Grandma was so excited that she sounded like a young schoolgirl.

"The doctor helped a little bit," I admitted, laughing. Then as I sat there in the hospital bed, nurses bustling about, and my husband hugging me, I explained how sorry I was that I hadn't been able to attend her special event.

She quickly shushed me, her voice catching as she replied, "No one could give us a gift that can ever compare to this. An anniversary baby is the best gift we could ever have."

A soft smile touched my face and I blinked back fresh tears. With my husband at my side, our child in my lap, and my grandmother's voice in my ear, I felt as if the best gift in the world had not been given to my grandparents at all, but to me.∼

Where I Belong

by Kim Peterson | *Monroe, North Carolina*

AS WE GATHERED AROUND THE NEW TOMBSTONE, tears burned in my eyes. I felt a wet drop slip down my cheek and turned my face toward the sun's warmth. I was crying for a man I never knew.

I looked at my mother, then to the matriarch of our family, my seventy-year-old Aunt Lula. They both sang with the people standing among the graves. I felt like I had come home.

My quest for belonging began seven months earlier, after my husband had researched his family tree. My husband met distant relatives online and over the phone. The family members decided it was time to gather the descendants of those Michigan Duryees. A reunion was planned summoning relatives from Canada and the United States. The Duryees were coming home to meet each other.

Impressed by the many stories he unearthed about these people and others, I wondered about my own family. Beyond my great-grandfather's name, I had no sense of our heritage or where we came from.

"I have no one who did anything back then," I complained.

My husband reassured me that even if my ancestors hadn't been major players, they had definitely lived some history, too. He searched the Web finding very few leads; then he discovered the Starnes Triennial Association.

STA members descended from Frederick and Mary Starnes, the family founders who came to America more than 330 years ago. They share research, maintain a quarterly newsletter and Web site, and assemble annually to meet extended family. As we clicked from page to page, we found that they had held their last reunion in Hickory, North Carolina. We had been an hour from their gathering while on vacation. Ironically, I had just missed meeting all of them. We scanned more pages and learned that they were next meeting in Monroe, North Carolina.

"You'd better go," my husband encouraged as he bought us an annual membership.

During the next six months, I uncovered some of my past, tracing our family back to Arkansas, Oklahoma, Tennessee, and into several counties in North Carolina. Those STA folks probably forked off the same branch six or seven generations ago.

When June arrived, my aunt and I drove from Indiana to Tennessee, where we picked up my mother. The three of us drove over the Great Smoky Mountains into North Carolina. As we approached the host hotel, we laughed and joked. We'd come a long way to spend a weekend with a bunch of people we had never met.

"We can always leave if we don't belong," we assured ourselves. After registration, feeling a little awkward, we joined "our family." Greeted warmly, we eavesdropped as people compared family genealogies. Our awkwardness slipped away that night when a local church hosted our first formal gathering.

Over a delicious Southern meal, my mom and aunt stared at our table partners. Finally, my aunt blurted to the bearded man across from her. "It's uncanny. You look just like my grandfather." Mom agreed. They felt an odd sense of having gone back in time eating dinner with the hero of their childhood years. Fortunately, Jimmy Starnes didn't mind the comparison, and we savored supper with his family.

Back at the hotel, melodies from a mandolin, guitar, autoharp, harmonica, and a homemade upright bass filled the lobby. Starnes families filled the chairs, the floor, and spilled into the hallway. An old-style Southern jamboree developed and music saturated the night. The hotel lobby resembled the porches of a past era.

The next day, our cars formed a caravan and we traveled to several family sites. I snapped photos of the marker erected in the 1970s commemorating the Starnes's arrival in the Americas, and then we visited a cemetery where Joe Carter found gravestones of his Starnes ancestors. Since he didn't have a camera, many of us took pictures to mail to him. We visited a Bible camp where a Starnes-owned cabin revealed some of our spiritual roots. We laughed and talked, and we enjoyed the discoveries. These people loved the present but celebrated the past.

One primary destination that day included a graveside memorial service and the dedication of a new marker. Now here I stood honoring Captain John Starnes, a Revolutionary War hero. As I watched my new family sing, I realized most knew the hymn by heart. The reading of Scripture and the telling of this soldier's role in history transported us through time. After the minister prayed, we milled around, touched by the sacrifice of one of our ancestors.

As we said our goodbyes later that day, I felt a sense of homecoming, and I knew I would be back. This was where I belonged.～

Buses, Trains, and Taxicabs

by Dorothy Read | *Gleed, Washington*

IN 1943, MOM AND I WERE WAITING OUT THE WAR, just like most folks who weren't directly involved in it. We lived with Grandma and Grandpa in Gleed, Washington, a small town consisting of little more than a cold-storage fruit warehouse called the Big Y, and a spur rail laid down to haul off the fruit. Grandpa grew the finest Bartlett pears in the Yakima Valley, everyone agreed. They even named our corner after him. "Megorden's Corner," they would say, "one mile due east of Gleed, kitty-corner from the Grange Hall."

Mom and I did our part to help out. She slopped the pigs, tended the chickens, and drove the tractor. In her spare time, she played a lot of solitaire. I harvested asparagus from around the fruit trees in the summer, raked leaves into great piles in the fall, crocheted headbands from rainbow skeins of leftover woolen yarn in the winter, and in the spring helped Grandpa stake out the quail nests on the orchard floor, so he wouldn't run over them with the plow.

Pop was in the navy. He was stationed in Norfolk, waiting for an aircraft carrier called the *Randolph* to be finished so that he could be sent to war. Uncle Don was in the army air corps in England, but he couldn't tell us what he was doing—it would have been censored right off the onionskin paper we used to write letters to and from the war zone. Every night after supper, Grandpa sat on the hassock in front of the Philco and listened to Gabriel Heater report the progress of the war. Mr. Heater brought the war right into our lace-curtained living room where Grandpa could fight it, too, with much head shaking.

Pop called one night in July to say the navy was sending him to aviation maintenance school at MIT. He asked Mom to come to Boston. We were astounded. So too, I expect, were the sixteen families on our party line.

At the grange potluck the next day, friends and neighbors whispered, "Margie's going to Boston." They dared not say it aloud, as it was contraband information. When she did announce it, she harvested a bumper crop of advice on travel and geography. Everything past Spokane, Washington, would be new territory for her, and travel was not easy in 1943.

A week later, Mom boarded the Union Pacific in Yakima with a ticket in her hand that assured her of a coach seat. As it turned out, she sat in the aisle on her suitcase all the way from Spokane to Boston, leaning against whatever uniformed shoulder was next to her when she needed to sleep. They didn't mind. She had given up her seat, as grateful civilians did in those days.

My grandparents and I met the mailman at the top of the driveway every day, and we were seldom disappointed. After Mom painted word pictures of the elegant house they shared with three couples, and the wondrous sights of cobbled streets and historic white-spired churches, she would write how much she and Pop missed me. I missed them, too, and cried a lot. I stared at the letters and repeated what Grandma had read to me, until I realized that I'd learned to read.

The asparagus turned to seed, and the leaves succumbed to autumn. Aviation maintenance school in Boston was over for Pop, but instead of coming home, Mom went to Norfolk with him. There she would stay until the *Randolph* was ready to go to war and take Pop with it.

Snow covered the fall-brown fields of the Yakima Valley. Christmas approached. Mom wrote about making a tree of green crepe paper for her hotel room and stringing it with popcorn-and-cranberry garlands.

I was glad she had a nice Christmas tree, but nothing at home was as festive as it should have been. The world seemed bleak with worry. I did not want my father to go to war, and I could not bear to think of Christmas without my mother. I spent hours on the laps of Grandma and Grandpa, crying and being comforted.

The day before Christmas, Aunt Ethelwyn, Uncle Merl, and my cousin, Phyllis, drove in from town, just ahead of a fierce snow-storm. They added their wrapped packages to the collection under the tree. I stroked and patted the colorful ones that had come from Boston and swallowed a lot to choke off my tears. Phyllis and I played Parcheesi, but without joy. Grandma served the traditional Christmas Eve dinner, but even pumpkin pie with whipped cream failed to lift my spirits. Eventually, it was time to hang stockings and trudge off to bed.

I was hugging Aunt Ethelwyn goodnight—a lingering hug because she smelled like Mom—when we heard a car turn into the driveway. Peering out of the window through the heavy snow, I saw a taxicab.

Not bothering with coats, we all tumbled onto the back porch in time to see Mom step out of the cab. In bare feet, I catapulted from the porch steps and into my mother's arms.

Grandpa invited the cab driver inside, and everyone laughed and cried and talked at once. Mom explained that the *Randolph* had not returned from its shakedown cruise, which meant it had probably gotten involved in some sort of war-related activity. Pop had sent her a telegram on December 19 that read, "Go home." My mother abandoned her crepe-paper tree and embarked on a 3,000-mile journey by any bus or train heading in a westward direction—the last seven miles by taxicab in a blinding snowstorm. It was an incredible feat at Christmas in wartime America.

"I don't know how you did it," murmured Aunt Ethelwyn.

Holding me tightly in her strong arms, my mother said, "I just told everyone who could help me, I have to get home to my little girl for Christmas." ෨

THE TOWN OF

Gleed, Washington

Population: 2,947

Town Facts

Original names • James Gleed, the area's first settler, examined his new homeland with the critical eye of a farmer. Sagebrush and barren, rock-covered soil met him on every side, and thus he dubbed his homeland Last Chance Valley. Often referred to as Lower Naches, the town was later formally named in honor of Gleed.

Location • Gleed lies approximately seven miles from Yakima, in the center of Washington State. Thirty-five miles due north is the town of Ellensburg. Another 100 miles west, over Snoqualmie Pass and through the Cascade Mountains, lie Seattle and Puget Sound.

Industry • In bygone years, small ten- to twenty-acre orchards coexisted with larger farms. Today, Gleed's fruit industry is dominated by mega-growers who supply a worldwide market. Well-tended orchards line Highway 12 between Yakima and Naches. A railroad spur line slices through the middle of Gleed, connecting the market with the huge cold-storage warehouses that dominate the little town and ensure continued employment.

Home Sweet Home

*I*n 1878, following fourteen years of service in the Union Army, James Gleed packed his wife, Sara, and their belongings and headed toward Washington to claim his soldier-earned homestead. Within three years, Gleed had surveyed and built an irrigation ditch for the Naches Canal Company and had grown Yakima Valley's first crop of alfalfa. When

Gleed discovered he could claim land by growing trees on it, he started the state's first timber culture, and received a deed signed by President Grover Cleveland. ✺

The Megordens of Gleed

*M*egordens don't live in Lower Naches any more. Nelle harvested one last bumper crop after Willis died in 1955, and then sold the farm, the home she loved for twenty-three years, and moved to "town" where she lived to be eighty-nine. Aunt Ethelwyn (Newbill), a spry ninety-four, lives in Yakima near her daughter, Merla (Thysell). Uncle Don (Megorden) returned safely after the war and migrated to the Seattle area. Marjorie and Dorothy welcomed Pop (Leonard Ainsworth) home; they moved to Seattle and later settled in California. Cousin Phyllis married Glen Blackburn, born and raised in Gleed, and they eventually made their home in Othello.

Dorothy Read writes, "Few Gleed residents remember 'Megorden's Corner' anymore. But family visits to Yakima always include a drive-by viewing of the old farmhouse, owned now by Keith Lawson, its lovely modern country look belying its age. Megordens have left, but we took with us years of memories of sunshine and laughter, tears and comfort, music and Christmas programs, and the kind of loving family solidarity that comes with growing up on a farm in small-town America." ✺

Reading, Writing, and Arithmetic

*T*he old Lower Naches School, serving all grades through high school, has been replaced by a modern multibuilding elementary school. Mrs. Pointer's one-room Gleed School, grades one through three, has been renovated into a gracious home on the Old Naches Highway. Its owner, Al Tinsley, makes popular wooden toys in his workshop and sells them in Seattle. His workshop has replaced the two-seated outhouse and the old playground that had once boasted an abandoned car chassis, perfect for little girls in an earlier time to use in playing house. ✺

The Wondrous Seashell

by Carol Kehlmeier | *Westerville, Ohio*

THAT WONDROUS SEASHELL looked down on me from the shelf. Inside the slick smoothness of its beautiful pink shell it held secrets and history from all of the family gatherings it had watched over the years.

"Pick it up and listen to it; hear God's ocean," Grandma would say as my eyes wandered to the seashell time and time again. I picked up the shell in my small hands and ran my chubby fingers over the knobby texture. Turning it, I peered inside to look for the ocean. I shook it, trying to get a drop of salty water to trickle out onto the worn linoleum.

The inside, where the shell rolled back, was pink and silky smooth. The rough outside was covered with different shades of natural colors.

"Like God's people," Grandma explained. I put the open side tight against my ear and listened. And I heard it—the roaring of the ocean waves.

The wondrous seashell was there for me when Pearl Harbor was bombed. When three of my uncles went off to war on the other side of the world, I held the seashell to my ear and listened.

The shell was there when Grandma hung the white-and-red banner in the window, emblazoned with its three blue stars. With the shell to my ear, I heard her pray for the safety of her sons.

It was there for the Thanksgivings, Christmases, and Easters without her boys.

Many times I climbed into the big overstuffed rocking chair with the shell in my hands and listened. Closing my eyes, I saw giant whales and sea monsters. And I saw God's gentle hands protecting Grandma's boys.

The seashell sometimes sat on the table in front of the window, the sun shining through the lace curtains, creating a halo around it.

"Is it from angels?" I asked.

"God made it," Grandma answered. I sat patiently holding the shell and waiting for my uncles to come home. And finally, they did.

The seashell was there for weddings, births, and funerals. It listened to family arguments. It heard apologies. It saw tears and laughter, hurts, healings, and blessings. It heard all of my secrets. It heard me sing and saw me dance. It listened to my made-up stories and songs. It heard me pray.

"It's the most beautiful seashell in the whole wide world, Grandma," I declared. "When I grow up I'm going to have one just like it."

"Oh, but it's the only one like it in the world," she answered.

Grandma was right. There is not another seashell just like it because this one was hers.

Today, the seashell is mine. Each time I take it up and listen, I hear the same sounds that I heard when I was a child in Grandma's living room: the muted sound of God's vast ocean mixed with the rise and fall of family voices. The seashell is familiar and soothing. It makes me feel safe. When I hold it to my ear, it takes me back to a simpler place in time, a time when family was everything, and I was never alone.

Tennessee Celebrations

by Elaine Young McGuire | *Donelson, Tennessee*

I WAS BOTH THE COUNTRY MOUSE AND THE CITY MOUSE during the holidays my family spent in Tennessee. We shared an extravagant Christmas breakfast with Mother's family—in a gorgeous, thoroughly modern home—before going to Grandmother Young's house, which had an outdoor toilet and coal-burning fireplaces.

In 1880, my mother's grandmother, Virginia Moore Miles, began to pen more than 100 years of family history. Her story started with the Moore family's arrival in Virginia, in 1760, citing stories from the Revolutionary War all the way to events a few months before her death, in 1890. In her own handwriting, though worn and faded, we can still read her words. "The ancestors of the Moore family . . . were noted for their hospitality, integrity, and great love for each other, virtues their descendants would do well to imitate."

Each year, on Christmas morning (except for the year my twin sisters had chicken pox), my family followed a routine. We got up early to see what Santa left. We opened presents and dressed quickly in our brand-new Christmas outfits. Then we headed to Aunt Estelle and Uncle Miles's house in Donelson, a sleepy little town near Nashville.

Our anticipation rose as each mile drew us closer to the Christmas morning family reunion. It was an unforgettable hour-long drive. We turned off the highway, drove past the little schoolhouse, across railroad tracks and toward a large stone house—where we turned right—and then straight to my aunt and uncle's new home. This new house was even more welcoming than their old log house had been.

Though it was Christmas, we never exchanged gifts. Our gift to one another was unconditional love. Excitedly, we ran up the front steps and straight into the arms of the first aunt, uncle, or cousin to open the door. Love enveloped us.

Our family numbered more than fifty before my grandparents passed on. After that, each branch of the family gathered separately with their own families. But that would come much later, after I married and moved away.

Back then, my first goal was to seek out my grandparents. Nanny and Dee-daddy were usually sitting in comfortable chairs near the fire. The mantle was tastefully decorated with fresh evergreens and an assortment of bronze bells from Switzerland, each topped with a red velvet bow. After sharing hugs and kisses, I'd sit down to visit for a while. Satisfied that I'd received a heaping helping of their love, I'd wander off to peek into the big kitchen, where the kitchen help, in their white starched uniforms, would be putting the finishing touches on the meal. Aunt Estelle and Uncle Miles would be right there in the thick of things, making sure everything was done just right. Before they had built their successful dairy business and could afford help, they had prepared the entire dinner themselves. I couldn't fully appreciate their effort until years later when I, like they, had four children of my own to care for.

The kitchen table was an informal gathering spot for those who could hardly wait for eggs to be scrambled and grits cooked. The large dining table was reserved for older family members, and card tables were scattered throughout the living room, den, and sunroom to make sure there was room for everyone. All of the tables were covered with starched white linen cloths and set with fine china, sparkling crystal, and elegant silver. A Christmas centerpiece and candle sat in the middle of each table, making the atmosphere almost magical.

Breakfast would be served at eight-thirty sharp. The call would ring out, "Breakfast is ready!" We gathered around, bowed our heads collectively, and thanked God for His Son, our family, and the bounty set before us. After we had eaten our fill, we wandered off to be with favorite cousins.

One fateful Christmas day when I was fifteen years old, my five-year-old brother, Gentry, disappeared with our cousin Stan. They were soon spotted walking on the thin ice of the lake. Our hearts stopped. Once the children understood the danger they were in, we were able to get them to lie on the ice and crawl back to safety. The entire family prayed during and after their rescue. This terrifying event reinforced what we already knew: Traditions are important, but faith and family are more important than everything else.

Much has changed since those Christmas days. Times are hectic now, and practicality has replaced formality. Each of the seven branches of Nanny and Dee-daddy's family celebrates the season with its own clan. With a slight twist, my family now shares the traditional Christmas breakfast on Christmas Eve. Aunt Estelle and Uncle Miles's gorgeous house was destroyed by fire, and Gentry died at the young age of forty-two. Stan and his family continued the dairy business with the same integrity my grandfather and uncle modeled. They have been blessed and now host huge Labor Day family reunions. More than 100 family members attend, and new cousins get to know one another each year.

Recently, I attended church with my mother and saw Stan's daughter in front of us, bouncing a beautiful baby girl on her shoulder. I smiled at the mother and child and embraced the knowledge that family traditions will continue, despite changing times and urban demands.

Long ago, Virginia Moore Miles gave wise counsel, and her family has heeded her advice. Love of family, integrity, and gracious hospitality still define us.⸮

Apple Butter Day

by Rachel J. Johnson | *Higginsville, Missouri*

The last Saturday in October provides my husband, two daughters, and me a chance to get out of the city. This day also offers an opportunity to participate in a generations-old family tradition. It's a time for good conversation with extended family members and a day filled with fun games and peaceful reflections.

Regardless of weather conditions, carloads of relatives and invited friends arrive at the Cunningham Farm in Higginsville, Missouri, at eight in the morning to set up for Apple Butter Day. We show off our family solidarity and educate the youngsters about this pioneer-type method of preserving, all the while helping them create lasting memories.

Grandpa Bruce and Grandma Helen invited me for my first taste of Apple Butter Day some ten years ago. I recall how I soaked up the peace of the day, taking it home with me. I've been back ever since.

Three years ago, we bundled in winter coats, braving the icy wind and rapidly falling snow. Huddled together near the fire under the shed roof, we made apple butter. Two years ago, we were in shorts and tank tops, trying to stay away from the fire, which added to the day's heat.

But last year, the weather was perfect. The sky was clear blue. The wind blew lightly, and we were comfortable in jackets. The preparation began as colorful leaves swirled around us.

We set up under a walnut tree. First, we made a circle with bales of hay, which doubled as a fire ring and as sitting space. Then, we carried firewood to the middle of the circle and built two fires.

Meanwhile, Grandma Helen and Uncle David cleaned the two huge black kettles with a mixture of vinegar and salt to remove any tarnish. They worked until the insides of the kettles shone like new pennies.

We use copper or brass kettles, not iron—that would turn the apple butter a greenish-gray. We also use hardwood stirring-paddles of hickory, oak, or walnut. Several half-dollar coins or marbles are always placed at the bottom of the kettles to prevent scorching.

Around ten o'clock, Mom and Uncle Bob added the ingredients.

For our twenty-four-gallon kettle, we add twenty to twenty-one gallons of applesauce, twenty-five pounds of sugar, one pound of cinnamon, and one pound of Red Hots. The cinnamon and Red Hots turn the apple butter a nice brick-red color. We add the ingredients accordingly for the smaller, twenty-gallon kettle, then settle back to stir and visit.

In the old days, people used apples rather than applesauce, but it took all day to break down the apples. Using canned applesauce, we only have to boil and stir for about four and a half hours. It has to be stirred constantly, so we take turns.

As we made our apple butter last year, the weather permitted us some fun. Around noon, we roasted marshmallows and hot dogs, ate homemade chili and potato chowder, and drank apple cider and tea. The kids rode the pony, and we all took turns petting sheep, cows, goats, and the numerous cats and dogs that played about our feet.

In keeping with the time of the season, a nearby car radio called out college football scores in the background. Later, many of us took time out for a quiet walk in the fields or forest to contemplate the winding down of another year.

We taste the apple butter and add more sugar or cinnamon until we are happy with the way it tastes. Then we use an assembly line to carefully dip the apple butter into jars, and seal each with a boiling hot lid.

The small portion left on the bottom of the pots is quickly gobbled up. Before we are finished, everyone has a homemade roll spread thick with fresh apple butter. After cleaning up, we check to see if the jars have sealed, and then make sure each family has a share to take home.

Our good weather last year continued into the evening, as the adults played Scrabble and bridge while the kids watched movies and frolicked in the house.

I wouldn't miss Apple Butter Day for anything.

Three years ago, Grandpa Bruce died. He was the one who taught me to play bridge and introduced me to the peace of Apple Butter Day. I feel his spirit with me every year on Apple Butter Day, and I remember to pass along to my children his wisdom of taking a day off for family fun.

The Crab Feast

by Ray Weaver | *Pasadena, Maryland*

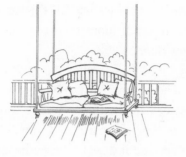

"Do they bite, Pap?"

My grandfather smiled brightly at my six-year-old cousin, Ricky. "Stick your finger there in the basket and see for y'self, boy."

It was the same answer he had given me a few years earlier. Pap was a big believer in "learning by doing."

It was a dumb question, really. Of course they bit—hard! Why else would Pap be wearing heavy, black rubber gloves in the soggy heat of a way-down-in-August Maryland afternoon? Even the ever-present Camel stuck to his lower lip looked sweaty as he pulled the Chesapeake Bay blue crabs from a wooden bushel basket and threw them into the stained steaming pot. Every once in a while, a sharp claw would work its way through Pap's glove, and he would refer to the crab in language little boys probably shouldn't hear.

Pap, my dad, his brothers, and I had crossed the Chesapeake Bay Bridge before dawn to crab a part of the bay we called Crab Alley, along Maryland's Eastern Shore. Some people did their crabbing from piers, with traps or hand lines, using chicken necks and eels as bait. To us, that was crabbing for city folk. We rowed our old wooden boat out to where the crabs lived, and then walked knee-deep in the briny bay water with bushel baskets floating in inner tubes tied to our belts. We flushed the crabs out of the seaweed with long-handled nets and scooped them up into the baskets behind us.

At daybreak, we realized we had hit the weather and tides just right. We managed to catch more than two and a half bushels of keepers within a few hours.

While the men were busy wallowing in Chesapeake mud, the women were busy at home covering the two big wooden picnic tables under the backyard oak tree with last week's editions of the *Baltimore News American*. They also carried the small breakfast table out of the kitchen and covered it up—that was the kids' table. A pile of mismatched butter knives lay on top of the newspaper, waiting. They were for cracking and picking the crabs. Some folks had actual crab mallets with little knives built into the handle, but we weren't quite that uptown on Mountain Road in Pasadena.

Before tossing the crabs into the pot, Pap placed a wire rack on the bottom and poured in just enough water and apple-cider vinegar to cover the bottom of the rack.

"We don't boil crabs in Mar'lin, Raymie, we steam 'em," Pap explained. "Boil 'em down in Virginia—ain't worth eatin'—damn waste of a good crab."

After each layer of crabs, he sprinkled in about half a cup of spicy Old Bay Seafood Seasoning mixed with rock salt. Pap liked his crabs spicy. When Pap was the cook, your lips burned while you ate.

Before putting on the lid, he looked around slyly and said, "Now, don't tell your grandmother." Then he dumped in half of a bottle of National Bohemian Beer. "Secret ingredient." He winked. "Now, get that on into the kitchen. We got two more pots left t' do."

A pot filled with big, hard crabs is a heavy load for a twelve-year-old boy, but I wasn't about to let Pap know, so I wrestled it as best I could up the back steps.

When my grandmother saw me coming, she yelled through the screen, "Herb, are you tryin' to give the boy a hernia? Here, Raymie, just set it up on the stove. Did Pappy remember the beer? Makes 'em taste better, so they say. I wouldn't eat one if you gave me money. Allus look like big ugly spiders to me."

When the blue crabs were steamed to a bright red, Pap put the kitchen radio in the window and tuned to WBAL and the Orioles. They were, as always, just a game or two behind the Yankees. (I hated the Yankees when I was a kid. Still do.)

As the steaming pots of crabs were dumped onto the newspaper, I took my place alongside my sisters and cousins at the kids' table. Along with the crabs, there were oleo-drenched platters of late sweet corn picked from the garden behind the house. There were Tupperware pitchers filled with sweet tea, steel coolers packed with ice, and Coca-Cola in little green glass bottles, the way Coke was meant to be. Some of the men had icy brown bottles of Natty Bo, which we older kids were always trying to sneak sips from.

Eatin' crabs is messy business. The women and girls wore sleeveless shirts and old shorts, and the men and boys got down to their cutoffs and T-shirts or no shirts at all. Everybody had his or her own way of picking and eating. My dad picked two or three crabs clean until he had a good pile of meat built up. Then he would butter a piece of bread and make a kind of crab sandwich. My mom liked hers with saltine crackers. I wasn't that patient. I yanked off the shell, carefully scraped out the *devil*, which, as every Maryland kid knew, was deadly if eaten. Then I cleaned out the innards, broke the crab in half, snapped off a back fin, and stuck the clump of meat straight into my mouth. I was good for a dozen fat ones on my own.

As with any great meal, steamed crabs take a lot of effort and a few hours to enjoy. We took our own sweet time, savoring His bounty and the perfect summer day He'd given us. Neighbors slowed down, honked, and waved as they drove by. We waved back, even if we couldn't tell right off who was doing the honking.

Around the kids' table, the talk evolved as we grew older. It was less about baby dolls and BB guns, and more about makeup and cars, cute boys and pretty girls, and Elvis. Rumor had it that my sister, Sandy, had been seen holding hands with a football player after Friday night's game. (I, myself, had been writing smoldering love notes to Kathy Williams. I tore them up as soon as they were finished, but I was writing them.) Soon, nervous, silent boys would appear next to my sisters and girl cousins, and nervous, chatty girls would be perched next to me and the other boys at the table, and our family gatherings would start to feel somehow different.

On this late summer's day when I was twelve, though, it was still just us kids, together for a little while longer at the kids' table, right next to and worlds away from our parents.

The lazy sun drifted west, the O's discovered yet another way to lose to the Yanks, and everyone ate their fill. If they didn't, it was their own darn fault, as my grandmother would say.

We cleaned off the tables, took the garbage down to the pigpen, and collected the few leftover crabs for soup the next day. We washed our hands in the freezing water from the hand pump at the well, and the finished the day's feast with a Popsicle. Soon, lightning bugs would appear, and we'd run through the cornfields and catch them in Mason jars, just to let them go again. The old house had no air-conditioning, so it was cooler outside, and even the grownups would stay out for a while on this night, sitting and smoking and talking grownup talk, until the mosquitoes finally drove everyone inside.∾

Cousin Jean

by Barbara Brady | *Des Plaines, Illinois*

I DIDN'T LIKE MY COUSIN JEAN. She lived in Chicago with her parents and considered me a small-town hick. They seldom visited, an arrangement that suited me just fine.

When Jean's family did visit, I had to wear the disgusting hand-me-down clothes that she brought to pass along to me. One of the worst offenses was her donation of appalling thigh-high, beige stockings. On cold mornings, my mother thought my skinny legs needed to be covered, so I was forced to wear Jean's hideous remnants of the Dark Ages. As soon as I got through the door, I rolled the stockings down around my ankles. Jean was thusly responsible for the ugly tire-sized rims above my shoe tops that marked me as a hand-me-down wearer and caused me to suffer total humiliation.

My two older sisters conveniently disappeared each time Aunt Laura and Uncle George arrived with our sissified cousin. I got stuck with her because we were the same age and because my parents insisted that I remember my manners.

Jean lived in an apartment in the city and didn't know how to do any fun stuff. She couldn't climb trees, ride a bicycle, or roller-skate.

◄◇►

Not only was she a complete blob of immobility, she didn't want to learn. The only thing she did with skill was stick out her tongue at me when no one was looking.

"Where's your record player?" Jean whined as she walked into my bedroom on one such hated visit.

"I don't have one," I replied stiffly.

"What? No records?" She folded her arms across her chest and heaved a sigh. Jean claimed to be madly in love with Mel Tormé, a popular singer of the 1940s. Apparently, a day without hearing him croon was sheer torture for her. I didn't want to confess I'd never heard of the Velvet Fog, as she insisted he was called.

Instead, I shrugged. "I don't like him." If this labeled me a small-town bumpkin, I didn't care.

Jean sat on the edge of the bed dejectedly. "Can't we go to the movies, then?"

Fortunately, our parents vetoed the idea, so I didn't have to risk my friends seeing me with my creepy relative. Jean moped around, pestered her parents, and grumbled, "What can I do now?"

Exasperated, Uncle George poked around in his pocket and pulled out a shiny fifty-cent piece. "Here, take this. Go to the store and buy candy for all the kids."

Fifty cents to spend on candy was a windfall. If I scraped together a couple of pennies, I felt rich. A nickel was wealth of astronomical proportions. For fifty cents I could tolerate Jean, even at the risk of being seen in public with her.

As we walked to the neighborhood grocery store, thoughts of jawbreakers, chocolate dots, BB bats, Necco wafers, and licorice whips thrilled my imagination. Jean hogged the fifty-cent piece, so I knew we would have to agree on the kind of candy to buy.

Inside the store, we hungrily peered through the glass case at the sugary display. "I like licorice," my cousin boldly announced.

"You do?" At last she spoke my language.

"Yeah. Let's get all licorice." Maybe my weird cousin wasn't from Mars after all. She actually liked licorice, my favorite candy.

We bought licorice cigarettes, licorice whips, licorice jellybeans, and Crows. I had always wanted a five-cent licorice cigar so we splurged and got several. We frustrated the grocer, but finally we had chosen at least one of every kind of licorice behind the candy counter.

Jean plunked down the fifty-cent piece and we each grabbed a brown sack bulging with goodies. We strolled home, leisurely devouring our hoard. By the time we arrived, our mouths were black as burnt wood, but our taste buds danced in delight.

My sisters moaned when we offered them pieces of the remaining goodies. I merely shrugged, already knowing they wouldn't like our choices. Jean and I went outside and sat on the front steps with our loot. The rest of the day passed quickly. Jean and I devoured every single piece of the licorice bonanza. Not even once did the ugly beige stockings cross my mind. I actually looked forward to another get-together with my new favorite cousin.

With my arm around Jean's shoulder, we leaned our heads together and began planning her next visit. I'd borrow my sister's record player, and she would bring her Mel Tormé records. Of course, we would need a new supply of licorice.ᴄᴡ

Aunt Clara's Tears

by Betty Downs | *Clyde, North Dakota*

WE GATHERED AROUND THE TABLE in the dining room of the farm-house near Clyde, North Dakota, where I grew up. We had just devoured one of Mother's famous fried-chicken dinners. I ran my hand slowly along the old linen tablecloth, crisp and white, marred only by a few coffee stains, and touched my fingers to the small holes Mother had expertly mended.

Grandmother, her soft white hair piled high, her sister Clara and her husband, Uncle Oscar, Mother in her blue-flowered print dress, and Dad dressed in the jodhpurs and the tall lace-up boots he was accustomed to wearing, all sat around the table with me. Heavy silverware gleamed in the noonday sunshine that streamed through the south windows. Crumbs from the spicy apple pie we had just enjoyed were scattered among the dessert dishes that remained on the old table.

Dessert finished, the family dinner was now in the talking and reminiscing stage, most interesting to my ten-year-old brain. Adults are funny people, I thought to myself. They always talk about the old days, back when they were children. I could see this occasion would be no exception. The black onyx clock sitting so regally on the shelf ticked away the minutes as I listened to the conversation around me.

Everyone at the table, except me, had been born in Illinois. Grandmother and Granddad had immigrated to North Dakota from Illinois in 1910, when my dad, their oldest son, was sixteen. Aunt Clara and Uncle Oscar still resided in Illinois, but they were visiting Grandmother as they did every fall.

Soon the conversation turned to the many Christmas seasons when Grandmother and Aunt Clara's parents, Tauder and Grammie, had opened their huge brick house to their five daughters and their families. Daughters, husbands, and children all moved in to spend the entire week visiting, cooking, and playing games.

It all sounded so grand. I could see the snowball fights, my dad as a boy, skating with his cousins, and my mouth watered thinking of the taffy pulls. I could feel the warmth from the candles on the huge Christmas tree that sat grandly in silence behind the parlor doors. Listening to their stories, I could almost taste the steamed pudding and cakes the ladies served to the joyous family that gathered around the table. I heard the shouts of laughter as they opened packages that contained pocketknives, scarves, and hair combs.

Aunt Clara, who was a beautiful lady, must have been visualizing it too, for to my absolute astonishment she suddenly began to cry. Mounds of wavy red hair surrounded her face, which was now wrinkled with sadness. Reading glasses, hanging by an ornate beaded chain, heaved to and fro across her ample breasts. Tears cascaded down her chin to drop onto her cream-colored blouse. Bejeweled fingers tapped on the linen-covered table as the tears streamed in rivulets down her rounded pink cheeks. Laughing and crying she looked at me and exclaimed, "I do believe I'm homesick!"

Never having seen my dear Aunt Clara cry, I didn't quite know what to do. I was amazed as I looked around to see my dad's eyes were moist, and Grandmother was dabbing at her face with a corner of her apron. I realized that for a brief moment, my dad was a boy again, and his mother and aunt, the two sisters, were reunited with siblings and parents they loved and missed.

At the time, I could not conceive why older people would cry for something that had happened so very long before.

Now, sixty years later, I close my eyes. I am back in that wonderful, warm, sunny dining room, sitting at that linen-covered table with my mother and father, my grandparents, aunts, and uncles. I smell the fried chicken, taste the apple pie, and hear again those wonderful stories told by those fascinating people I love and miss. Tears stream down my wrinkled cheeks. I do believe I'm homesick! ✍

Farmhouse

by Gayle Sorensen Stringer | *Tyler, Minnesota*

It was as cold as a Minnesota winter, that Minnesota winter. Two days before Christmas, my husband and I, and our nine-month-old son, sped up the desolate spine of I-29 from Kansas City due north—home to Tyler.

Cold and bleak. On either side of the highway, depleted corn and soybean fields stretched to the gray horizon. A sorry splattering of snow paid lip service to winter, barely covering the dark, frozen soil. Weary corn stalks, left ravaged by the picker, leaned this way and that. In many fields, the plow's final word echoed in large, black lumps. The nation's heartland: resplendent in the season of growth and nothing short of dismal in December.

"I just hope we can make it in time." I spoke the same phrase my husband had heard repeatedly since we had gotten the call from Mom.

"He's really bad," she'd said. "Please come. I think he's waiting for all of you."

My grandpa, Clarence Skjong, was a southwest Minnesota farmer. He was Norwegian and English, Lutheran, the father of seven children, and the grandfather of fifteen. His wife, Mary, had suffered from multiple sclerosis for over twenty-five years. So had he.

His life was simple by most measures, but rich beyond those measures. He understood the value of hard work, the promise of a man's handshake, and the solace of faith. And even in the midst of hard times, the spring in his step and the twinkle in his clear, blue eyes were as constant as hope itself. Those of us blessed to call him "Grandpa" knew the true meaning of unconditional love. Somehow, he made each of us feel like "the favorite."

We always gathered around him and Grandma. While most of our aunts, uncles, and cousins had dispersed to other parts of the state, my four siblings and I were fortunate to grow up on a farm just four miles from our grandparents' home. In spite of the distances, the whole family gathered frequently and for any excuse. Holidays, birthdays, and vacations almost always found the adults around the Skjong dining room table, talking, laughing, and playing games, while the grandchildren banged in and out of the house, no matter the season or the temperature.

The original two-story farmhouse was old. Enclosed porches poked from the front and the back, and the cellar was entered through an outside lift-up door. I suppose the house was quite small, but to my child's eye it seemed massive with a kitchen, dining room, living room, bedroom, and bathroom downstairs, and four bedrooms and a storage room up the creaky wooden staircase. People today would probably say it had character. All we knew was that that house and that farm were the best places to play in the whole world.

As they always do, times changed. Given Grandma's wheelchair restriction, the farmhouse was eventually sold and moved to another location, and a modern ranch-style house became the family's new gathering place.

We grandchildren began growing up and exploring lives of our own. Grandma eventually succumbed to the strong will of her disease. Grandpa sold most of his farmland to my father, but he helped with the work as much as possible. Slowly, our gatherings grew fewer and further in between.

When we reached Sioux Falls, South Dakota, that frigid December 23, I called Mom. "He doesn't seem conscious, but I know he's holding on for all of you to get here," she said. "Please hurry."

A battle raged within me during those last 90 miles. I wanted to get there, and I didn't. I wanted to see him, and I didn't want to see him. Finally, we pulled into the parking lot of the small Tyler hospital and found our way to his bedside. A congregation of friends and relatives spilled into the corridor, but I don't remember their faces. All I remember is his labored breath and his frail hand in mine.

"We're all here now, Grandpa," I whispered.

He died shortly after our arrival.

Two days later, we gathered at the farmhouse for Christmas. Despite our grief, we knew what we must do—carry on. So we exchanged gifts that bitter Christmas Day. In each individual's pile of unopened presents rested a small, oddly shaped parcel. Absentmindedly, I picked mine up and read the label. "It's from Grandpa!" I cried.

All of Clarence Skjong's children and grandchildren rummaged through their own piles and pulled out similar packages. In a flurry of festive paper and ribbon, we unwrapped our gifts. Inside, we each discovered a clay ornament adorned with a hand-painted image of the old farmhouse.

"Dad had these made for you by a local artist," my Uncle Ron said. "One way or another, he wanted to be here this Christmas."

Twelve years have passed since our last farmhouse Christmas.

But when I hang that ornament in a place of honor on my own family's tree each year, I know that we are all gathered. And I hear Grandpa's chuckle one more time. ↪

THE TOWN OF

Tyler, Minnesota

Population: 1,218

Town Facts

First incorporated • Tyler was incorporated in the summer of 1887, and the town was named after C. B. Tyler, a well-to-do area businessman.

Location • Tyler is tucked in Minnesota's southwest corner, on Highway 14. It lies approximately 40 miles west of Walnut Grove (home to Laura Ingalls Wilder from 1874 to 1876 and again from 1877 to 1879) and three hours west of Minneapolis–St. Paul. The area is surrounded by thirty lakes, many of which are called "kettle" lakes, created by depressions formed under the glacier thousands of years ago during the last Ice Age.

Transportation • Tyler has a small, municipal airport, but most people travel to and from the town by car.

Industry and Recreation • Agriculture is the dominant industry. Farmers grow cash crops of corn, soybeans, and wheat, and/or they raise livestock. Some dairy operations also exist. A variety of small businesses can be found in Tyler, ranging from grocery stores to the city newspaper. Tyler also hosts a small hospital, an eighteen-hole golf course, a municipal swimming pool, a bowling alley, an ice rink, several parks, and a city library.

The Skjongs of Tyler

Most of the seven Skjong children and their families have dispersed to other regions of Minnesota or other states. One son, Ron, and his wife, Carla, aunt and uncle to contributor Gayle Sorensen Stringer, settled in Tyler to raise their four children. Carla manages the city library and Ron is involved with the Catholic Youth Program. ∾

A Town Destroyed and Rebuilt

Nearly the entire town of Tyler was destroyed on August 21, 1918, at 9:20 P.M. when a tornado touched down. Once the dust had settled, many of the buildings were no longer standing. Additionally, thirty-three lives were lost. Building debris was found as far as 23 miles outside of the town boundaries. ❧

Unique Characteristics

Velkommen to Tyler, Minnesota, home of the *Nissemaend* (Danish elf) and the *Aebleskiver* (Danish pancake)! Tyler's strong Danish heritage makes it unique. In 1884, Lutheran church authorities throughout the upper Midwest put their heads together with the railroad company and created a contract to set aside some 35,000 acres of land around the Tyler area. The catch was that this acreage was to be sold within a three-year period, to Danish immigrants only, for $3 to $8 per acre.

To provide Danish immigrants a place to live in their new homeland, the Danebod Lutheran Church and Folk School were established in 1886. The Folk School concept was developed by N. F. S. Gruntvig, a bishop and member of Denmark's parliament. The Folk School eventually closed due to lack of funding, but Danebod's Folk School and Lutheran Church are now on the National Register of Historic Places.

People continue to travel across the United States to use the Danebod facilities for summer family camps and for various conferences and meetings throughout the year. Danebod remains a vibrant hub for the community. ❧

Summer's Dance

by Virginia Rowledge | *North Stamford, Connecticut*

EVERY YEAR IN THE MONTH OF JUNE, my family would pack our clothes for the move from our eight-room colonial. Down the dirt path, past pear and apple trees and past the chicken house, acres of growing vegetables, the bright patch of zinnias, marigolds, and snapdragons, we moved over the brook to our three-room cottage in the woods. For the entire summer, strangers from New York City lived in our big house, used our best dishes, slept in our beds, and had parties with their friends from the city. We made the move because Mom and Dad needed the rent money, but my older brother, Donald, and I thought of it simply as the perfect summer adventure.

At the cottage, we carried water from the brook to wash clothes, dishes, and ourselves. We bottled drinking water in cider jugs from the outside spigot at the big house and brought them to the cottage.

Mom, a pioneer gourmet, used a kerosene stove and wood-burning oven to cook, bake, and preserve vegetables, pickles, and fruit. The bottles of green beans, tomatoes, and peach halves glistened like jewels on the shelf in the cellar.

The outhouse was down a path at the back of the cottage, near the woodshed. Going to the outhouse at night proved to be a very scary trip. Spiders and wild animals might be lying in wait to get us. Mom and I always went together, singing or whistling and shining our flashlight beam far ahead to scare away snakes, skunks, or whatever. We used the china pot under Mom and Dad's bed only on rainy nights.

Donald and I usually went to bed before the sun went down, so there was time for Mom to read to us from our favorite book.

On one special night, Mom allowed Donald and me to wear our Sunday school clothes and stay up after dark for a family party. Mom lit kerosene lamps on the tables and on top of the upright piano. Then she put dishes of chips and little cream cheese sandwiches on the painted table next to the orange zinnia bouquet.

Donald and I stood on the front porch in the twilight, watching and waiting. From afar, we heard car doors, laughter, and talking. Our many aunts, uncles, and cousins walked through the picnic grove, over the weathered log bridge, and up the path of stepping stones, their lights bouncing up and down under the oaks like beacons.

Our cousin, Marthanne, was the first to arrive. She bounded up the steps, shined her father's big silver flashlight in my eyes and yelled, "I'm here." Then she twirled into the house, banging the screen door.

My aunts wore printed dresses and looked and smelled like a flower garden. My uncles had on clean shirts and shiny shoes. They carried rolls, watermelon, tuna-macaroni salad, baked beans, and a chocolate cake. They placed the food and some wrapped packages, for Mom and Dad's anniversary, on the table near one of the lamps, and sat down around the room on couches, chairs, and my brother's daybed.

A damp breeze entered our cottage windows as I pressed my nose against the lower screen. I peered into the night and saw the fireflies flash to one another in the dark woods. I heard the night bugs' fiddle, louder than the human voices.

Enjoying our time together, Marthanne, Donald, and I tossed a beanbag back and forth until Mom stopped us. "Not in the house," she said with a slight nod toward the door.

With his pointy ice pick, Dad knocked pieces of ice from the block behind the top door of the icebox. He filled jelly glasses with ginger ale and ice chips for the children. Then he used a doll-sized measuring glass to add liquid that smelled like cough medicine to some of the glasses he then handed to the adults.

Marthanne and I sat at my tea table. Donald spun around on the piano stool, going higher, then lower. Mom brought our icy glasses to us. The ginger ale tickled my nose and I giggled, my brother and Marthanne laughing with me. Donald was tall enough to reach the handle so he wound the Victrola, set the needle, and looked very proud as the music began to play.

As the sounds poured from the Victrola, I held my ear against the side of the cabinet and listened to the beat in the heart of it. Dad must have felt it too, for he set his glass down, pushed the rag rugs aside, and grabbed Mom. He held her close and twirled her around the room. She blushed and laughed when he whispered something in her ear. Their shadows danced on the walls, giant ghosts in the yellow light. My aunts and uncles sang along with the record, "Let me call you sweetheart, I'm in love with you."

Just then, my favorite uncle held out his hands. I unbuckled my black patent leather shoes, held my arms up to reach his big hands, and stepped onto his polished wingtips. Atop his strong feet, I danced like Cinderella. Marthanne watched, wishing for her turn. The music slowed. My brother was busy eating potato chips and drinking more ginger ale and had forgotten his job.

When the music stopped, Uncle Bert bowed and thanked me. I grasped the edge of my skirt, curtsied, and burst into tears—I was having so much fun, I had wanted that dance to last forever!

Soon, Donald danced with Mom while Uncle Bert cranked the Victrola. Much later, Mom cut the cake and we all sang "Happy Anniversary." I waved to Marthanne as everyone departed, until I could no longer see her on the pathway. It had been a good party.

The cottage was small, the furniture secondhand—before shabby was chic—but stars shone on its roof and moonbeams lighted the rooms that night when we went to bed.Ꮻ

Homecoming

by Carol Burnside | *Jeddo, Texas*

DADDY'S SIDE OF THE FAMILY had a special gathering of relatives and friends they called "Homecoming." Not that very many of the people attending this annual event actually called Jeddo, Texas, home. According to my sources, the dry spot along that dusty Texas road know as Jeddo could only claim seventy-five residents in its entire population from 1939 to 1990.

All I ever remember seeing was the cemetery, a long stretch of highway, and so many people my mama said you "couldn't stir them with a stick." Why would anyone want to, I wondered? And where did they all come from? I knew how they got there. Cars and trucks of the 1950s and early 1960s lined the road and spilled into the yard adjacent to the cemetery.

They came from Waelder, Rosanky, Gonzales, Lockhart, and San Antonio—or, like us, Mineral Wells or places even farther away. Some came from—gasp—other states! (Traitors. Everybody knew Texas was the only good place to live.)

There were six of us in my family: Mama and Daddy, my two older brothers, Jerry and Billy, and my older sister, Sue, and me. To

◄○►

get to Homecoming, we piled into our ugly green Chevy wagon—already loaded to the gills—and spent the next four hours driving in the scorching summer heat.

We liked to get there early to camp before and after the event. Homecoming, and the importance of extended family, was still a big thing in the early to mid-sixties. We camped at Daddy's "old home place." This illustrious description was attached to a stretch of green outside Uncle Raleigh's cow pasture upon which Daddy had built a rather large steel and aluminum shed. We slept there, ate there, played, and sweated there. Mattresses were rigged on platforms and lowered down with pulleys when needed for sleeping. They fit snugly along the wall at other times. An outhouse was available for "visiting Mrs. Jones."

Mama would tie tumbleweeds together tightly around a stick and sweep the place out, getting rid of spiders, mouse nests, and such. Water, cold and thirst-quenching, was drawn from the well for washing and cooking. God forbid that we might arrive too many days before the Homecoming. That would mean washing our hair on Saturday night, and Mama had too many kids to waste time heating water.

On Sunday, primped in my exquisite homemade dress, replete with pin tucks, lace, and a starched petticoat, I'd offer my face—shiny from being scrubbed clean—for inspection. Then we'd all squeeze back into the Chevy and head for the white one-room church in the middle of nowhere. It was supposed to be fun, and it was, even though the day included a hot church service and visiting the flower-laden graves of the dearly departed.

Once the last amen had been said, Mama hurried to join others in laying out cloths on the tables lined up under huge tarps strung between trees. Food appeared like magic, until the tables all but disappeared. Ice dumped into large washtubs housed glass bottles of Orange Crush, Grapette, Coke, and root beer. Gallons of iced tea, lemonade, and Kool-Aid sat atop the refreshment tables.

Given that I was a young kid at this event, I don't remember the hard work that went along with the festivities, but I do remember the second cousins and great-great-aunts performing the clichéd cheek-pinching ceremony, and the comparisons that followed. Whose ears, nose, and eyes had I inherited?

Today, I close my eyes and remember the aroma of damp talcum powder and sweat. I visualize wrinkled red lips homing in on my cheek and feel again the suffocation of being squished against a massive bosom: Aunt Maryanne—my grandpa's aunt—and her bright floppy hats, with brims so wide they created shade. At least we could see her coming and dodge the inevitable for awhile.

My own children haven't the sense of familial history that I carry within me from events such as these, for changing times and the need to repeatedly uproot ourselves ensured they never experienced them. They don't have that sense of history, steeped in overtold stories and the fact that you have your daddy and grandma's ears.

But I write these things down for them, in hopes that someday my stories will mean a smidgen to them of what they have meant to me.

And while I write, my heart is rejuvenated, for I am transported back in time to a dry spot along a dusty Texas road. The place is called Jeddo: So many people are gathered there that you couldn't stir them with a stick.✐

Little Boy Lost

by Pat Capps Mehaffey | *Stamford (Jones County), Texas*

"COME SIT BY MY BED, CHILD, and I'll tell you about the time we lost your brother," said my elderly mother. Her eyes were glassy with a faraway look that seemed to come over her at odd times. "The year was 1930. You were a little baby and your brother, Jimmy, had just celebrated his fourth birthday. That was long ago, but the scenes from that day stand sharp and clear in my mind. I even remember the clothes people wore and the food we served them."

I watched my mother's face and smiled softly. Though she was unable to recall clearly what had happened yesterday, some twist of memory function allowed her to remember the days of her children's youth. She looked at me quizzically with faded brown eyes. Did I want her to go on with the story? I nodded, and she continued.

"My mother had died one year previously and my father had recently suffered a stroke. Paralyzed on one side, he was deeply grieved and depressed. I tried everything I knew to cheer him. I helped him out onto the porch every day after breakfast so he could enjoy the morning-glory blossoms and the hummingbirds. He sat there with tears falling down his cheeks. I cooked his favorite foods and he dutifully tried a few bites, but obviously felt no pleasure. Sometimes, late at night, I heard him moaning softly in his room. Even the antics of four-year-old Jimmy brought him no joy. Finally, unable to think of anything else to try, I took my worry and anxiety to my older brother, Art.

"Art, deep in thought, paced the floor back and forth then said, 'Dad has six brothers and one sister, all of them still living. He has seen one or two of them from time to time, but I know they haven't all been together for thirty years. Why don't we plan a family reunion for them?'

"That sounded like a great solution and I enthusiastically agreed. We decided on a two-day celebration, with some of the festivities at my home and some at Art's farm. I volunteered to get addresses for all the honorees and send a letter to each of them.

"Soon, replies began coming in from Oklahoma, New Mexico, and many places in Texas. All of the siblings planned to attend and would bring their children and grandchildren with them. Each one expressed pleasure at the prospect of being together again and several offered to bring money to help with the cost of the food. We expected seventy-five to eighty-five guests.

"Art and I started issuing orders for both our families at each party site—much work and preparation needed to be done. Carpenter's sawhorses, with boards laid across them, were set up in the yards at both homes. Covered with old quilts, these would be the serving tables for heaps and mounds of food. All available chairs and benches were placed under the trees. Barrels of water and tubs of ice would be needed at both locations. We determined to serve breakfast at my home and have lunch and supper available at Art's. We even assigned little Jimmy many chores.

"As the reunion date approached, our stoves were in constant use as we whipped up three-layer cakes, pies, fried tarts, and big batches of cookies—jobs made more difficult because of Jimmy's hungry and continual presence in the kitchen.

"In the early morning hours of August 22, 1930, far-flung family members started arriving. Those living nearby came in wagons pulled by teams of horses. Many drove up in Model T cars. Some traveled by train and were met at the railway station. By late evening, a total of ninety relatives were in Art's yard holding plates piled high with food.

"By midnight, many were sleeping on beds or pallets in one of our homes. Others slept in their cars. The overflow made do with bedrolls or cots in the open air.

"The story-telling, political arguments, and loud discussions among these gregarious, vocal, opinionated, loving individuals continued throughout the following day intermingled with the consumption of food. The whole while, Dad smiled, talked, and even laughed out loud.

"In the late afternoon of the final day, after long, tearful good-byes and words of gratitude and appreciation, the visitors began to leave. When the last car departed, the massive job of restoring the yard, privy, barns, and houses to normalcy commenced.

"We all worked hard for an hour or so, pleased that the party had gone so well. Suddenly, someone asked, 'Where's Jimmy?' Every possible place was searched; we called his name repeatedly. Art's wife even checked under the beds and in the closets. Soon we faced the heart-chilling fact that Jimmy had disappeared.

"Frantically, we looked in the barns, hay bins, storage sheds, even the stock pond with no results. At last there was no place left to search—that's when we heard the sound of an automobile chugging down the dirt road toward our gate. We went out to meet the vehicle, hoping they brought the news we wanted to hear—that they knew where Jimmy was. The car stopped in front of the gate and one of my uncles got out holding Jimmy. 'I'm so sorry,' he said. 'I know you were worried about him. We traveled 30 miles before we discovered him asleep on the back seat. I wish we could have brought him back sooner.'

"Light-headed and dizzy with relief, I grabbed Jimmy and stood there beside the car crying and hugging my uncle. I've never forgotten that fearful span of time when I thought my only son was lost, and you were destined to be an only child."

When Mom finished speaking, a faint smile touched her lips. That faraway look still gleamed in her eyes, but I knew—at least for now—the story had ended. I smiled and got up from my chair to fluff her pillows and lightly touch her cheek.

Right then, at that very moment, we were content. I could fill in the blank spaces of what had happened today, for her, and she could fill in the blank spaces of long-ago happenings, for me. Things would change, I knew, but for that brief moment, we had all we needed.✍️

A Need for Independence

by Nancy Jackson | *Gleneden Beach, Oregon*

THE RED-WHITE-AND-BLUE FLOAT ROUNDED THE CORNER, followed by a bevy of people in costumes. We hollered and whistled, waving our hands in hopes that candy and treats would be tossed our way. After the year we had gotten squashed too far back to have a good view of the parade, my family and I always headed out early in the morning to reserve a premier spot. I loved this day and never hesitated to show it. I would thrust my miniature flag high into the air and sing/shout, "My Country 'Tis of Thee," until the rest of the family joined in. There was no other way to start the Fourth of July than the Gleneden Beach community parade. A love of tradition has never ceased in this small coastal town in Oregon.

On each Independence Day, fancy, old-fashioned cars in mint condition were polished to perfection, and their drivers drove them in the parade, honking antique horns. Firemen flashed their lights, and the whir of sirens filled the crowded streets. Pets were decked out in whimsical attire. Children rode bicycles decorated with colorful streamers and pom-poms. Clowns handed out balloons, the "tidy maids" walked along, cleaning up after the horses and dogs, and everyone cheered.

Many people came out to root for their fellow companions. Even the tourists gathered to watch, quickly caught up in all of the enthusiasm. Local figures from businesses, resorts, hair salons, and more walked the parade route, smiling and waving to their supportive residents. It meant a lot to see the folks who filled our gas tanks, bagged our groceries, and put on the nighttime firework display having a great time. Somehow it only increased the respect and adoration for our modest community. On this day, we were all family. If you blinked you would miss us, but on the morning of the Fourth, you'd think our town filled all of the Pacific Northwest.

The Fourth was a day we looked forward to, a time we dressed in patriotic colors, with jackets in tow and pocket change for popcorn, peanuts, and hot dogs. We stood around and talked to other family members and anyone else who was near enough, glancing down at our watches every few seconds, waiting for the parade to begin. American pride could be heard for miles, or at least that's what we told ourselves.

After an hour or so, the final police car flashed its lights, a signal for us to clear the streets in a safe and orderly fashion. Roadblocks were removed, and we walked back home, adrenaline pumping through our veins. Dad started the barbecue, and for the next couple of hours, my family gathered to feast on hamburgers, hot dogs, my mom's famous potato salad, chips, and some sweet treat or another. Beneath the sunflower-colored umbrella on the picnic table, we laughed and chatted the time away. Our conversations ranged from which was the favorite float and costume to who had the most impressive car.

By mid-afternoon, Dad would be snoring in his easy chair. The clatter of dishes indicated Mom was cleaning up. I did my best to stay occupied. I couldn't wait for evening to arrive so that we could head down to the pier behind Mo's restaurant.

After dinner, my spirits soared. We grabbed sweatshirts, rain jackets, and extra socks. Armed with blankets, soft cushions, umbrellas, and our added clothing, we looked like vagabonds. We picked a nice open spot in the sand, not too close to anyone, and stared up into the dark night sky. Each year, somehow, we lucked out. The rains stayed away and let us enjoy our annual celebration. With one loud fiery red blast, the thrill of lit skies and brilliant colors began, and they kept me awestruck for what seemed like hours. One after another, the bursts of blue, gold, pink, and green danced over our heads and rained down in shimmering streaks and swirls. We clapped after each one to let our appreciation be heard. The grand finale, the most stunning display of them all, was always met with the most rousing applause. With the smell of a campfire in our hair and tiredness that comes from having totally enjoyed yourself, my family headed back home, nodding to our friends and neighbors as we passed.

I'd hum "My Country 'Tis of Thee" until I was tucked beneath the sheets, the vision of dancing lights still in my head. I'd hope for another year to go by fast, so I could see a new float round the corner, and I would hold my flag high in honor of our great little community of Gleneden Beach. ◌

Saturday Night on the Town

by Jacquie McTaggart | *Strawberry Point, Iowa*

"George," my mother said to my father, "you'd better go out to the barrel by the garage and put some gas in the car. I noticed it was running low when I took the apples over to Hilda's today."

My dad, dressed in his best blue bib-overalls, didn't bother to remind Mother that it was illegal to "barrel gas" for anything other than farm machinery. He didn't have time to remind her of the stipulation, and he was in no mood to argue. He was excited about the prospect of showing off his brand new 1959 Chevrolet Impala, and eager to hit the road.

My folks had purchased the car earlier in the week, and Dad knew that it would be the envy of every person in Strawberry Point—all 1,232 of them. That baby was low, long, wide, and curvy. It had batwing rear fenders, wild tailfins, cat-eye tail lamps, and a huge deck lid. Its $2,592 sticker price seemed small for such a thing of beauty.

As usual, we were going to spend Saturday evening in the nearby town where both my parents had grown up, and where we were on a first-name basis with every man, woman, and child. After filling the gas tank, Dad gave three loud honks to let us know that his mission was completed and he was raring to go.

Mom, my sister, Marilyn, and I quickly scampered to the car and climbed in. We were also eager to get going because we wanted dibs on the number-one Saturday night parking spot—the southwest corner at the village's lone intersection, directly in front of the wooden four-by-six-foot structure that served as a popcorn stand. That particular location was premier, because everyone passed by it and stopped to visit at some point during the evening.

The fourteen-mile ride into town that night was especially jovial. Dad was driving his "I-have-arrived" vehicle. Mom was wearing her almost-new housedress, and twelve-year-old Marilyn was looking forward to meeting her friends at the movie theater for a rerun of *Lassie, Come Home*. Me? I was looking forward to the treat that always served as the culminating activity for Saturday night—an ice cream sundae.

Although she was invisible, Lady Luck must have accompanied us that evening. Despite running a few minutes late, our coveted parking space was still open when we arrived at the corner popcorn stand. As Dad was wheeling his new "boat" into place, Mom outlined the familiar Saturday night rules and regulations.

"Marilyn, here's fifty cents. This will pay for your movie ticket and some popcorn. Now remember, you are not to sit in the balcony. That's where the big kids go, and you're far too young to get big-kid ideas. Remember, we will all meet at Podendorf's Drug Store at exactly nine o'clock. I expect you to be on time."

Marilyn grabbed the half-dollar, muttered thanks, and took off running toward the Orpheum Theatre. I'm sure she never heard one decibel of Mother's warning to "Slow down and walk like a lady."

Dad, who was starting to get edgy, was next. "George, you're going to the pool hall to play huckly-buck, right?"

Dad looked at her impatiently. "Maybelle, you know full well that's where I'm going. Isn't that where I go and what I do every Saturday night while you and Jacquie do the grocery shopping?"

Mom agreed that it was, and then proceeded to remind him, for the 999th time, how important it was for her to know the whereabouts of each family member—at all times. Dad sighed, said that he understood, and started to walk away. Suddenly, he stopped, turned back toward my mother, and said, "What happened to the weekly sermon about having only one beer with the boys?"

Mom smiled and replied, "This is a banner week for you. Go ahead and have two if you like. We'll see you at Podendorf's in a couple of hours."

At that point, Mom took my hand in hers and said, "C'mon Jacquie, let's you and me go to the market. We'll find out who's getting married, who's going to have a visit from the stork, and who has the most beautiful, smartest grandbaby ever born."

As I walked toward the store with my mother, I never thought to wonder why she didn't even mention the task of buying groceries. I was too busy admiring her beautiful cotton dress, feeling the warmth of her hand, and reveling in the fact that I was her special Saturday night companion.

When Mom and I walked into the drug store later that evening, I glanced at the Big Ben clock on the wall—directly above the soda fountain. The time was 8:58. We were actually two minutes ahead of time, and Marilyn was waiting for us at a table for four. We joined her, and waited for Dad. Nine o'clock came, and there was no sign of him. By ten minutes after the hour, mother was shifting from side to side in her chair and clearing her throat. At 9:15, she stood up and announced, "Girls, we'll wait in the car. I suspect your father may have exceeded his two-beer limit, and I refuse to be embarrassed in front of the townsfolk. We'll have to skip our Saturday night treat this week."

As we rounded the corner where our car was parked, we immediately saw a great number of men gathered. Some were looking under the hood, one was lying flat on his back staring up at the undercarriage, and others were simply stroking those grotesque tailfins.

Mom, forgetting to walk like a lady, ran up to Dad. "George, what is going on? Where have you been?"

Dad grinned. "Shucks, Maybelle. I was just showin' the fellas our new buggy. C'mon, let's take the girls and go get one of Podie's super-duper hot fudge sundaes."

Marilyn and I strolled along the sidewalk happily, thoughts of hot fudge sundaes in our heads. I glanced back at our parents to hasten them along, and grinned. Their step was unhurried and the look on their faces engaging. It was obvious from the shy smile on Mom's face that she was not upset with Dad, and from the way his arm wrapped around her shoulders, I think he finally understood why it was important to her to know where her family was at all times.

Welcome to the Family

by Al Serradell | *Guthrie, Oklahoma*

I GRIPPED THE PHONE TIGHTER, stunned by the caller's terrible news.

"Our . . . home," Jenny managed between sobs, "it's . . . gone. Burnt to the ground."

After several moments, she calmed down enough to give me the details. The night before, the family had a backyard cookout. Afterward, they had gone inside to watch home movies filmed a month ago at Jenny's college graduation. Jenny thought the fire must've started around midnight when the wind knocked over the barbecue grill, spilling hot coals onto the back porch.

Jenny's daughter had been asleep, but Jenny and her husband Carl had managed to pull her out in time. A close call, I thought, too close.

Sadly, Jenny's cocker spaniel, George, didn't get out. He must've gotten confused in the chaos. No ordinary family pet, the eighteen-month-old puppy had been a wedding gift from Jenny's kids for her and her new husband. That canine ranked up there with the family heirlooms, which also had been destroyed.

It was like losing all sense of the past, she later told me. No physical links remained to attach to the memories.

The loss was especially hard on Jenny. That house—her home—had represented freedom to her. Part of the divorce settlement from her first husband, the place also symbolized her painful odyssey from child-bride to mature woman.

I shared in my friends' grief. After all, Jenny and Carol had helped me through my allotment of tragedies, such as my mother's recent death from cancer. They'd even accompanied me to the funeral, not to mention all the cooked meals Jenny had brought to my home in the weeks following the tearful event.

Our closeness also sprang from a common denominator—the three of us worked at the same university. Carl served as manager of the financial aid department, while Jenny and I toiled in the public relations office. But perhaps what really connected us was the fact that I had introduced the two during a rehearsal of the school's spring pageant. Somehow, I just knew they would hit it off.

Their home also held special memories for me. I had been privileged to enjoy their lovely dwelling on several occasions, from dinner parties to lingering treks through the lush wooded area that surrounded their house. For me, the place boasted a reflective quality. I loved to sit on the back porch on warm summer evenings and watch the sun dip, pink and hazy, across the treetops, my mind lost in nature's tranquility.

After talking to Jenny, I spent the rest of that Saturday afternoon in shock and despair. After all they had done for others, Carl and Jenny didn't deserve this.

Finally I called my father, who lived 60 miles away in the small town of Duncan, Oklahoma. Before he had a chance to ask me what was wrong, I told him about my friends' disaster and that I felt so helpless. I also said I couldn't make the family reunion scheduled for the next day. How could I act happy and carefree when my two best friends had lost everything they owned?

Dad, who had lived alone since my mother's death, recalled the many kindnesses Carl and Jenny had shown the family during Mom's illness. "Don't worry about a thing, Son," he said. He then told me to bring them to the reunion. He said he thought they needed to be with family now.

"And don't take no for an answer," he added. "They're coming if I have to go get them myself."

I wanted to laugh at my father's infectious spirit. But how could we expect them to celebrate after such a tragedy?

Still, I went to the hotel where my friends were staying and told them they'd been invited to a family gathering the following afternoon. As expected, convincing them to join us proved a Herculean task. Neither of them wanted to be around people. All they could think about was what they'd lost, all the years of hard work and memories taken from them. But being my father's son, I refused to give up.

"I'll be bored without you guys there," I lamented. And then I explained that their presence was required—Dad's orders. "Hey, welcome to the family," I added.

Jenny laughed, the first time in almost twenty-four hours. I think that's what convinced them to go.

The mood in my car was somber when we arrived at the park for the reunion. That mood was about to lift, however, for no sooner did we step out of the car than we were bombarded with an outpouring of love for Jenny and Carl. My family had outdone themselves. Everyone had rifled through his or her own belongings, finding extra treasures to share. Some brought necessary household items, from a coffeepot to baskets of soap, while others presented boxes of food and clothing. There was even a small television set and an electric razor, plus a sizeable monetary donation. So much stuff had been collected that Jenny and Carl had to rent storage space until they could find a new house.

But the best gift came when Dad presented Jenny with a puppy. "He's just a mix," Dad explained. "Saw him at the pound and thought he needed a good home." ⌒

Silvertone Memories

by Amy M. O'Quinn (as told by her father, Edward
McIntyre) | *Irwinville, Georgia*

"COME ON, MAMA," I called over my shoulder. "We're gonna miss
some of the show if we don't hurry." I raced out the door ahead of
my parents and jumped into our old Chevrolet without a backward
glance. I was too concerned with my own thoughts at the moment
to notice the worry lines etched on Mama's face or the way Daddy's
strong shoulders slumped.

All I could think about was getting to my cousins' house for the
highlight of my week. We'd worked hard every single day, and now
it was Saturday night. Time for the broadcast of the *Grand Ole Opry*
on WSN Radio, live from Nashville, Tennessee!

We lived on resettlement farms that had been part of a
Depression-era government program known locally as the Irwinville
Farms Project. And since Wilbur and Carrie's place was nearby, the
drive took only a few minutes. I'd chattered all the way about Roy
Acuff, Ernest Tubb, and Minnie Pearl, and when the car stopped
I hopped out and took off running to find my cousins Eugene and
Jessie Mae.

Even though our families often traded work during the week, Saturday nights were extra special. We couldn't wait to sit around the Silvertone radio, sipping iced tea and eating teacakes Mama sweetened with cane syrup. Maybe Cousin Wilbur would even let me be the one to hook up the battery to the radio, which stayed disconnected during the week to save battery power.

I turned around to remind Mama to bring in the teacakes, saw her face, and then I remembered what, in the excitement, I'd forgotten. Yes, I was a little boy caught up with little boy thoughts, but I understood the reason for her sadness. I understood why we'd left church when the Western Union man brought the telegram the Sunday before. And even in my young mind, I understood why the grownups spoke in low tones about Hitler, Germany, and planes being shot down. My only brother was now missing in action and we had no other information, only hopes and fears.

I'd even heard the hushed whispers not meant for my ears, before we'd left home, but I hadn't really paid attention to the bits and pieces.

"Stay home . . . Don't feel like going . . . No, it'll be good for us to be around family . . . The young 'uns enjoy it . . . Okay, we'll go."

The key word I'd heard was "Go," and I was ready. But at that moment after I had gotten out of the car, I could see how sad Mama was as she followed me into Carrie's kitchen. Now, looking back across the years, I know that she and Daddy were also determined. Determined to keep going, determined to trust the Lord to keep my brother safe and bring him home again, and determined to keep family life as normal as possible.

And family was what those Saturday night visits were all about. We'd sit around that old radio, laughing, singing, and clapping to those songs of long ago. We just enjoyed being together. During work and play, bad times and good times, we were there for one another. The *Grand Ole Opry* broadcast provided one more opportunity to visit and make precious memories, even when the rest of our world seemed to be falling apart.

When the radio was finally hooked up and switched on, Minnie Pearl's "How-dee!" resonated across the miles through those magical airwaves. Mama's tired eyes lit up as she laughed, and Daddy's twinkled as he tapped his foot to Roy Acuff's "Wabash Cannonball."

After seeing their familiar and reassuring smiles, all was made right for a little farm boy in southern Georgia. It was a glimpse of how happy our lives would be again, when the war was finally over and my brother returned home. Because deep in our hearts, we had to keep on believing that before too long he'd be back in our family circle, listening to that Silvertone radio, and laughing and clapping right along.

THE TOWN OF

Irwinville, Georgia

Population: 10,060 (Irwin County)

Town Facts

First Incorporated • Irwinville (Irwin County) was named in honor of Georgia Governor Jared Irwin (1806–1809). The town was originally incorporated on December 22, 1857, and served as the county seat from 1831 to 1906, when it was moved to Ocilla. Currently, Irwinville is unincorporated.

Location • The town is situated in south central Georgia, on State Highway 32, about 20 miles from Tifton and U.S. Interstate 75; approximately 160 miles southeast of Atlanta, 150 miles west of the Atlantic coast; and 2.5 miles east of the Alapaha River.

Industry • Irwinville's industry is primarily composed of a large pecan buying/processing operation, a farm-supply business, two peanut-and-grain businesses, a cotton gin, a convenience store, a berry farm, three beauty shops, and a trucking business. Local farmers also raise livestock, but corn, peanuts, and cotton are the primary crops.

The McIntyre Family of Irwinville

*M*cIntyres have lived in the Irwinville area since the late 1800's. And in 1937, Edward McIntyre's parents, Neal and Ina McIntyre, were selected to be a part of the Depression-era Irwinville Farms Resettlement Project. Descendants still live on the farmstead, and farm the same land. Most of the family members have stayed in the local vicinity, and all are involved in the community events and activities. Those who did move away enjoy coming back for a visit whenever possible.

Civic activity is very important in the family. Most McIntyres are very active in churches as members, church leaders, and there's even a pastor in the family! Descendants of the McIntyre clan also include a bank vice president, farmers, teachers, homemakers, a nurse, a machinist, a law enforcement officer, federal employees, business owners, artists, and writers. ᴏᴠ

Famous People

A team of young basketball players, called the Irwinville Farmers, was known all over the state in the 1940s and early 1950s for their winning record. When they won their state championship in 1951, the *Atlanta Journal* claimed the victory as their seventy-third win in a row.

Coach Wallace "Country" Childs took this handful of untried farm boys and transformed them into state champs. He was inducted into the Georgia Sports Hall of Fame in 2003 with a lifetime coaching record of 512–111. ᴏᴠ

Civil War History

*I*rwinville was the site of the last major event of the Civil War—the capture of Jefferson Davis, President of the Confederate States of America. Expecting defeat, Davis and his party left Richmond, Virginia, heading toward Mexico. His escape route brought him to within one mile of Irwinville on the evening of May 9, 1865. Unbeknownst to Davis, regiments from both the Wisconsin and Michigan cavalries were preparing an ambush. Sadly, neither regiment was aware of the other. In the foray, two Union soldiers were killed. On May 10, Davis, fearing for his wife's safety, surrendered peacefully.

A monument honoring Davis rests on the capture site as part of a thirteen-acre Jefferson Davis Historic Site. Built in the 1930s, it was added to the Georgia Parks System in 1941 and includes a marker commemorating the deaths of the two Union soldiers. ᴏᴠ

A Little Piano Music

by Barbara Beaudoin | *Chelmsford, Massachusetts*

DID ALL LITTLE GIRLS IN THE 1940S HAVE PIANO LESSONS? It certainly seemed that way. Most of my cousins had to learn to play a musical instrument, and most of them actually enjoyed it. Nevertheless, one year of piano lessons when I was eight years old did nothing to nurture my very latent musical talent. I did learn to read music, though not to play it well.

My appreciation of all kinds of music grew through the years. My cousin Mike's teenage band allowed me to listen to their practice sessions. I thought they could play "In the Mood" better than you-know-who—but remember, I was only nine at the time. As teenagers, my friends and I played our records at one another's homes. In our imaginations, we sang and danced our way through Hollywood musicals and were certainly as capable of a hit recording as any of those girls who accompanied the famous bands, weren't we?

Everyone grows up eventually. When I did, I married, and my husband and I raised a family of five children. I sang and danced my way through housework, entertaining whichever infant or toddler was in the playpen at the time. I must have been truly inspirational because they all insisted on playing a musical instrument in the school band. My family contributed the sounds of drums, flute, and clarinet to the school concerts for many years, and our neighbors were treated to some great rock 'n' roll when my sons and their friends evolved into teenage versions of cool musicians.

When my first child was a young teenager, I had an incredible urge to have a piano in the house and diligently searched the classified ads to find one that was affordable. One day, there it was: an older upright piano, $500, and—what luck—only two miles from our home. The owner was a middle-aged woman who said she did not enjoy it any more now that her children had grown and moved away. She said it was just taking up space in her living room, and she hoped that we would have some fun with it.

We purchased it and had it delivered to my living room. I practiced and practiced—straining to remember what little training I did have. I listened intently to recordings of professional pianists, and strove to imitate their light and elegant fingering. Of course, I could not.

When Christmas arrived, we were happy to have a piano to gather around. We sang carols, as I had done years before around my grandmother's piano. That holiday was just as I had always imagined our family Christmas should be.

On birthdays, I played "Happy Birthday" and we sang the familiar tune and enjoyed the fun. So what if I missed a note or two, and if some of us were not quite the altos or sopranos we tried to be? Through the years, every family gathering gave us the opportunity to play the handsome upright and laugh at ourselves. In the process, the children grew up.

They fell in love, married, had children, and became very busy. And I was home alone with my piano. I tried to play it once in a while. The grandchildren would bang on it when they visited, and the neighborhood children couldn't resist it either, but it just didn't sound the same.

When it was time for my husband and me to leave our home and move to a smaller place that would be easier to manage, I struggled with the idea that I could not take my piano with me. I offered it to my children, but no one wanted it enough to arrange for the difficult move. So I placed a classified ad in the newspaper, just like the one I had read many years ago.

I received a telephone call from a prospective buyer, who sounded shy but excited. She came with her young son and daughter, and her father, who had chosen her first piano when she was a young girl. She loved my piano and bought it immediately. Apparently, the look on my face told her that I would be lonely without it.

She was a wise and thoughtful woman who knew that it was difficult for me to let it go. She took the time to explain that her daughter was studying the violin, and that she wanted to provide piano accompaniment. I could see many enjoyable hours ahead for them as they played their lovely music together, and I sensed that my piano would find a new home with a considerate and appreciative family.

But still, when the movers came and took my piano, I was lonely. Then today, I received a card in the mail with the following handwritten note:

> *Thank you for the nice piano. It helps my daughter practice violin. Your husband may find that he misses your piano. I think your beautiful piano sound will remain in your husband's heart and in the piano forever.*
>
> *May God bless you and your family.*

The note warmed my heart. I am happy now, knowing my special piano will continue making music for many more family gatherings.

Things Money Cannot Buy

by Joan Clayton | *Melrose, New Mexico*

I LIVED WITH MY GRANDPARENTS in a little town where doors were never locked. Everyone was trusted and seemed like family. When neighbors came to visit, Granny went to the door smoothing down her apron, which was covered with straight pins from her quilting frames.

I was astounded by Granny's ability to remember everyone's name and how she kept track of everything that was going on in town. I later learned her funny-looking wall telephone was the secret behind how she got most of her information. Her telephone signal was two short rings and one long, but I quietly listened to every call that came in on that phone, regardless of the ring, and heard a lot of things I probably shouldn't have.

"Child, don't you know that's not nice?" Grandma asked, and then quickly added, "What did they say?"

Granny was the heart of our family. She was always in the thick of things and made sure to start early in the year getting ready for the annual Christmas family gathering. Entertaining the families of my nine cousins required lots of preparation, so I did what I could to help her. I'm sure I hindered more than I helped, and as I think about it now, I can only marvel at the enormous amount of patience she always had with me.

One summer, Aunt Opal came to help Granny with vegetable canning. We washed and peeled the produce and sterilized the jars in big pans. I got so hot in that boiling kitchen that I persuaded Aunt Opal to sleep on a pallet outside with me that night on Granny's soft green grass.

We laid there watching the stars, a cool soft breeze lulling us to sleep. About midnight, something growled and started running toward us. We both screamed and ran to Granny's front door. I got there first, and in sheer fright shut the door in front of Aunt Opal. She stood there screaming. But instead of a wild animal, Granddaddy appeared on the porch behind her, laughing hysterically.

"Did you girls get scared at something?"

My mouth dropped open. "Granddaddy, it was you all along!"

We decided we didn't want to sleep outside after all and returned to our beds. I fell asleep to the sound of Granddaddy's muffled laughs coming from the other bedroom.

That adventure was soon put behind me. I was too busy counting the days until Christmas. The day Granny started baking sweet potato pies I knew it was getting close. I still remember the cake cover. It sat on top of the old wooden icebox. Many times I pulled a chair up so I could reach the lid and smell Granny's pies.

In those days, Granddaddy ran a filling station. And to our dismay, every Christmas Eve he stayed open until ten or eleven o'clock, in case he encountered weary travelers who needed fuel to make it home in time for Christmas.

Meanwhile, my nine cousins and I fretted, whined, and some of us even cried. "How many more hours is it?"

"Will we ever get to open presents?"

"Why does Granddaddy have to do this every Christmas Eve?"

"Let's just open one—he won't care!"

But every year Granny said the same thing. "Not without Granddaddy!"

So we waited and waited and waited. Finally, we heard his footsteps coming up the path. We whooped and hollered when Granddaddy walked in and took his seat in his favorite chair. Looking back, I remember Granddaddy never opened his few presents. But he sure loved to see us open ours, laughing all the while.

The gifts were inexpensive little things, but to me they could not have been better. One aunt gave me a little bottle of Chamberlain's hand lotion. It made me feel so grown up. Granddaddy and Granny always gave each one of us a sack with an orange in it, which was a rare treat for us. Finally, the relatives wished us "Merry Christmas," and left with a promise to see us on the morrow for the Christmas meal.

"Granny, could I sleep under the Christmas tree with the lights on?" I asked.

"No child, but you can sleep on the couch by the tree. The floor is too hard."

I fell asleep with the wonderful smells of sweet potato pies and roasting turkey filling my nose, and dreams of sugarplums dancing in my head. I truly thought I was in heaven. To my surprise, when I opened my eyes the next morning there was a present under the tree for me.

"I saved it for this morning," Granny said. "Since you're my only granddaughter, I thought you might like to have a *girl* present. I hope you like it."

I tore into the package as fast as I could. When I opened it, I almost cried for joy. There lay the perfect gift for a little girl: a tiny cedar chest, with gold hinges and a lid that closed tight, something just right for storing secrets. It was the best Christmas day of my life.

And the day just got better and better. Before lunch, a multitude of aunts, uncles, and cousins arrived with armfuls of food. I remember the special moment when Granddaddy said the before-dinner prayer. His voice broke, and I knew that Granddaddy meant it when he said. "Lord, we're so thankful for family, but most of all we're thankful for the Christ child." During the meal that day, a knock on the door interrupted our family time. A poor family's old Model T had broken down and they needed Granddaddy's help. He did not hesitate to leave his warm home and dinner table to go into the snow and cold to help another family. Now, when I think about it, I realize that my grandparents' unselfishness and love for each other touched many lives in that little town where everyone seemed like family.

Many years have come and gone since the family gatherings of my childhood, but over the years, one great truth—of which I am very proud—still remains in my heart. My family gave me things money cannot buy, and for that I will always be grateful.

Clearview Christmas

by John R. Bradley (as told by Lola Mae Bradley
Empson) | *Clearview, Tennessee*

THE YOUNG CHILDREN HOVERED around the pot-bellied stove, anxious to go home, as their parents told and retold tales of past Christmases. Older children congregated by the new dresses, which hung in a neat row by the front window. But no one would leave John Armstrong's country store until Mr. Armstrong gave out apples and candy at the end of the evening.

Armstrong's Store was the center of commercial activity in this rural Tennessee community. Whether a customer needed a new wool jacket or a side of bacon, Armstrong's was the place to go. Long before the time of modern-day department stores that also sold groceries, Armstrong's selections included clothes, food, even furniture.

Clearview families had gathered at the store on Christmas Eve for as many years as anyone could remember, but this tradition meant little to the youngest children. They knew that Santa could not visit their homes until they were tucked into their beds. Their patience wore thin.

Lola Mae Bradley tried to console her six-year-old brother, Lawrence, by explaining that it was still early. Seeing that her words made little difference, Lola Mae leaned in close and whispered, "I'll make sure we go home before Santa comes."

"But we might miss him. We need to go now," Lawrence pleaded. Looking around the big room, he found his older brother, Wayne, and solicited his help. "Come on, Wayne," he whispered. "Let's get Daddy to take us home."

"Be patient, Lawrence," answered Wayne. "You won't miss Santa." Then he added, "Of course, *you* may not get anything, anyway."

Lawrence didn't let the teasing get to him, but neither did he give up his single-track thought. "Please, let's go," he pleaded.

As the evening progressed, games were played, stories were swapped, last-minute gifts were secretly selected, and anticipation grew. Times were hard in the country in the winter of 1927, but farm families were thankful for what they had and enjoyed the festive holidays.

Finally, Mr. Armstrong distributed his Christmas goodies, and the families slowly dispersed. John and Bessie Bradley collected Lola Mae, Wayne, and Lawrence, and bundled them into their old Ford. Though the trip home was less than a mile, there was still much skill needed in order to negotiate the icy roads carefully in the still night.

As they drove toward their farmhouse, John teased his youngest son. "Lawrence, I sure hope you don't get a bundle of switches this year. I've sure been worried about you."

Lawrence drew his brows together. "Daddy, you know I've been good—especially the last few days." A hopeful look crossed his face as he glanced out the window into the gathered darkness. "I really think I'll get a new bicycle."

"Don't be silly," said ten-year-old Wayne. "You don't even know how to ride a bicycle."

"Yes, I do," Lawrence replied hotly. "Besides, I need a bike to learn how to ride."

"Wayne, stop picking on Lawrence," said Lola Mae.

Lola Mae was a sophomore in high school and felt she had to help her parents with the boys, whether her help was actually needed or not. She was not nearly as excited about this Christmas as her younger brothers were. Fact is, given the family's limited resources, she expected little in the way of gifts. But even if she didn't get any presents, she still looked forward to tomorrow's Christmas dinner with her family, which would include her grandparents, who lived three miles away.

As soon as they arrived home, Lola Mae and her parents helped her younger brothers hang their stockings by the chimney. Soon the boys had hurried upstairs to bed. Lola Mae helped her mother with the final Christmas Eve preparations before she too climbed into bed.

The next morning, Lawrence awoke early and quickly roused Wayne. Before going to the fireplace to check their stockings, the boys raced to Lola Mae's room. Soon all three were clambering down the stairs.

As soon as Lawrence peeked around the corner, he cried out loudly, "There's a bicycle!" He raced to the bicycle, not knowing how to ride it but determined to learn.

Wayne found several books he had wanted, along with a fancy Swiss pocketknife with all the accessories. Pleased, he took his time examining his new treasures.

But of all the children, Lola Mae was the most surprised. She found a beautiful Bulova watch and an Atwater Kent radio. She was astonished. The watch was unbelievable enough, but the radio! No one in Clearview owned a radio.

Without delay, she rushed into her parents' room. "How could I get such expensive gifts?"

John Bradley looked at his pretty teenager, a proud glint in his eye. "I got paid for the tobacco crop last week, and your mother and I agreed this Christmas should be special for you. You help us so much with the boys, and we want you to know we appreciate it."

Lola Mae, overcome with gratitude and love for her family, hugged her dad. "You should not have spent so much money on me," she whispered, wiping the tears away. "I sure do appreciate it." She strapped the watch to her arm, and then helped her mother prepare for the feast to come.

When the grandparents arrived, the family sat down together to enjoy a sumptuous Christmas dinner. Throughout the afternoon, the family enjoyed a new treat—listening to Christmas carols on Lola Mae's new radio.

Every so often, Lawrence would ask, "What time it is now, Lola Mae?" And Lola Mae was only too pleased to answer.

At the end of the day, Lola Mae said a prayer thanking God for her blessings, especially for the perfect Christmas Day. She had asked for nothing, but had received the most wonderful gifts. In addition to the watch and radio, Lola Mae had received the best gift ever, one that could never be wrapped and put under the tree. She had received and recognized the value and strength of a loving family, and there is no dearer gift than that.

Never Say No to Nina

by Trish Ayers | *Farmington, Illinois*

IT WAS THE SUNDAY AFTER THANKSGIVING, and my college boy-friend, Shan, and I were going to visit his family for their annual spaghetti dinner. We had less than a mile to go, and I was nervous.

We pulled up to a green ranch-style home just as a train, loaded down with coal, clattered past on the nearby railroad tracks. The sound mimicked my heartbeat, which was nervous and jumpy. Cars lined the street and filled the driveway. It looked like the entire town had been invited.

As we walked toward the house, the front door was flung open and Shan's relatives poured out to give hugs and kisses. When we finally got inside the house, there were more hugs and kisses. Aunts, uncles, and cousins were standing and sitting everywhere, and appetizers were placed on every flat surface. I finally found an empty seat beside Shan's great-grandma, Seconda, whom everyone called Nina.

Nina looked at me, then at Shan's Aunt Rosie, and said something in Italian. Aunt Rosie immediately hurried toward me with a small plate laden with goodies. Nina pointed to a cookie, "That's a *sucadini*, tastes like licorice." She waved her hands in an upward motion, "Eat it."

I loved red licorice, so I took a big bite. It was flavored like black licorice! I politely finished the cookie, washing it down with a big gulp of water. As soon as I had eaten everything on the plate, someone else handed me another plateful. Before I could refuse, Nina spoke with her thick Italian accent: "Eat. You're too skinny! You might blow away."

Shan smiled and snatched the *sucadinis* from my plate as he led me to the basement where the men milled around a bar decorated with Grandpa Fogliani's medals and ribbons from World War II.

Soon it was time to eat. As we crowded on the stairs beside Shan's brother, Mitch, he looked at me with serious eyes. "Do you like chicken gizzards?"

"No," I answered in surprise. From the way the men all looked at me, I should have suspected something, especially when Shan quickly intervened.

"We all like them," he said. "Don't worry."

I sat down in the closest chair, and Shan's cousin, Darci, grabbed the seat next to me. Mitch, Shan, and Shan's father, all scrambled to sit around me.

When the bowls where passed, Shan's dad heaped my plate full. I took one bite and to my surprise, uncovered a gizzard. Suddenly, forks from every direction dove toward my plate.

Mitch laughed. "Next time you may want to get your hand out of the way." I heeded Mitch's advice.

Toward the middle of the meal, Grandpa Fogliani stood up. The room went silent. He smiled, and said, "It's time for Christmas money!"

I watched in awe as he handed out fifty-dollar bills. Then he reached into another pocket and removed a wad of ten-dollar bills and handed me one.

"I can't," I said.

Shan noticed the exchange and leaned toward me. "Take it or it will insult him."

"Thank you," I said as I accepted the money.

Then Nina handed out five dollars to every grandchild.

Once the money was all handed out, conversations resumed, and everyone returned to their plates with renewed energy. After dinner, the women collected the dirty plates and returned with chocolate and lemon meringue pies. Nina was given first pick and then the guests. I selected chocolate, and kept a wary eye out for forks as I ate. Everyone laughed.

"We don't normally steal bites of pie," explained Shan as he gulped down a big bite of lemon pie from his own plate. "But, if you want, I'll be glad to," he added playfully.

When dessert was over, the guys disappeared while the women cleaned up. I tried to help but was told that guests weren't allowed in the kitchen. Seeing that I was a bit lost, Nina invited me to sit down beside her. As I took the chair next to her, I recalled Shan's words. "Nina is the matriarch of the family, you never say no to her."

"What part of Italy are you from?" Nina asked.

"I'm not Italian," I answered.

"Yes, you are!"

Before I could set the record straight, Shan came in and rescued me with an announcement that we needed to get back to college before dark. We tried to duck out quickly, but Nina called, beckoning me back. Discreetly, she handed me a five-dollar bill. I started to decline, but remembered it would be an insult. So I accepted the money and hugged her.

We walked out of the front door followed by all of his relatives. Nina walked up to me, pointed her finger into my face, and said, "You marry Shan and have a fifth generation."

Startled, I just stood there. Then Shan whispered in my ear, "Say yes."

I whispered back, "No."

The silence grew and finally Shan urged me a second time to say yes.

Talking just loud enough for Shan to hear, I ground out the word, "No!"

But Shan was adamant. "What Nina wants, Nina gets. Just say yes so we can leave."

"Yes," I quietly answered with the whole family as witnesses. Nina clapped and kissed us on both cheeks. We got into Shan's car and drove away waving and smiling. As soon as the house was out of sight, my smile disappeared.

"You told me it was a *small* family gathering!"

Shan held his hand up defensively, "It was for us."

"What about Nina's proposal?"

"It was kind of funny."

"Funny?" I squawked. I was ready to fight, or at least let Shan know how I'd felt when I'd been cornered into saying something I wasn't ready to say. But, as luck would have it, at just that moment, he smiled. I've never been able to stay mad when he smiles.

All these years later, I have to admit that Nina did know what she was doing. This year Shan and I celebrated our twenty-fifth wedding anniversary. We have two lovely daughters—our family's fifth generation—who both are well acquainted with the wonderful story of how their great-great-grandma Nina proposed for their dad.

Homemade Ice Cream at Grandma's

by James E. Tate | *Stillwater, Oklahoma*

LATE ONE SATURDAY AFTERNOON IN 1932, Grandpa brought home a block of ice from Stillwater, the town not far from his 160-acre homestead, and invited the family over for homemade ice cream. The summer sun was low in the Oklahoma sky as Grandpa set straight-backed wooden chairs in a shady part of the yard.

I watched excitedly as my dad, Frank Tate, and Uncle Willie Florer broke up the ice into small chunks and fed them into the large wooden bucket around the two-gallon pail of ice cream fixins, while Grandma poured salt onto the ice. My brother, John, brushed a long lock of white-blonde hair from his eyes and asked, "Why are you salting it?"

Grandma looked up. "It makes it freeze faster. Ain't you ever seen ice cream made before?"

John didn't answer. But he did sneak a piece of ice to munch on, as did my cousins, Billy and Wayne. Meanwhile, Grandpa put a gunnysack over the freezer and looked at me. "Jimmy, how about you sit on the sack to hold it down while we turn the crank?"

◄◦►

After a few minutes it felt cold, but I was in a perfect position to sneak a piece of salty ice so I didn't complain.

From my spot on the freezer, I watched Mom and my sisters bring out small bowls from the story-and-a-half unpainted frame house. They walked across a dirt yard. Grass or no grass, this was the ground my grandparents had driven their stake into during the Land Run of 1889, and we all were mighty proud of it. Their covered wagon had jostled them mercilessly in the rush to find free land. Once claimed, the land had to be "proved up," including farming and building a house during the first five years, or it reverted to the government. It was a grueling test for them, working from can-see-to-can't-see, and even later. At the end of the proving period, they had built their house, a barn, and several sheds, and they'd planted forty acres of corn and twenty acres of cotton. Their hard work had paved the way for luxuries like taking time out of a busy day to make homemade ice cream.

While the ice cream was being created, we kids grew more and more anxious. Once in a while, the grownups added ice and gave one of the other kids a chance to sit on the gunnysack, which was okay with me, since my bottom was getting wet. Finally, the ice cream freezer squeaked and slowed as it completed its task.

After we had each eaten several helpings, Grandpa leaned back in his cane-bottomed chair and began telling stories.

He cocked an eyebrow at us. "You kids think it's hot this summer? Why you young whippersnappers don't know what hot weather is. Back in nineteen-ought-three, it was so hot and dry that the fish came up from the creeks and ponds to live in our well. At suppertime, we'd lower the well bucket and bring it up full of fish. Sakes alive, the cows coughed up enough dry corn shucks that year for us to stuff all of our straw ticks with."

As we laughed, Billy teased Grandpa in return. "Oh, Grandpa," he said. "You're just making up one of your stories." Grandpa laughed louder than any of his four grandsons in response to this.

Finally, when all of the ice cream was gone, John, the oldest boy there, had an idea.

"Let's go down to the bridge!" he said excitedly to us kids. The Council Creek Bridge was close by in a holler surrounded by tall trees and spooky shadows, and was especially frightening in the dusky light. As we four boys drew close, John said, "Shh! I'm getting a funny feeling. They say this bridge is haunted."

Wide-eyed, Little Wayne asked, "What do you mean, haunted?"

John answered, with conviction, "Evalena said she saw something dark under the bridge. She thinks it's a troll!"

"A troll?" Billy asked.

"Yes, and it may grab us."

Suddenly, John jerked around and stared hard at the bridge. "I heard something under there. Let's get out of here!"

We ran back up the dirt road like cats being chased by hound dogs. But even before we got back into the yard I could hear fiddle music and felt reassured that no troll could get me if I was in the safety of Grandpa's music.

Uncle Willie was singing an Irish song in his baritone, complete with interesting facial expressions, while Grandpa played the fiddle. We all clapped hands when he finished.

"Lizzie, why don't you sing that Native American song, 'Naponee'?" Grandma asked my mother. Mom knew hundreds of songs by heart and it didn't take much coaxing for her to sing while we boys scrambled for more pieces of ice to crunch.

Before we knew it, the sun had lost itself behind cedars, elms, and scrub oak trees on the western horizon, leaving the family under twinkling stars. Mosquitoes moved in with the cooler air, so Grandpa started a fire to smoke them out.

There was nothing easy in those days, but looking back, I can honestly say I enjoy reliving every sweet memory as much as I enjoyed making them. ᡣ

From Grave to Cradle

by Suzanne LaFetra | *Glendora, California*

I watched over my aunt's shoulder while she patted my grandmother's forehead with a damp washcloth. In the carved cherry-
wood bed under the rose-print flannel sheets I had given her for
Christmas last year, my grandma laid, frail and scarcely breathing.

Family began pouring in from across the country. Her sister
from Oregon. A son from Chicago. Grandchildren from all across
California. Neighbors and a lifetime's accumulation of friends called
and came to the door, bringing roses, speaking in low voices. Grandma's immediate family huddled together in the living room, our faces
creased with worry, bunches of tissue wadded in fists and pockets.

I straightened the pink towels in the bathroom and heard my uncle
talking on the phone to his employer, his voice catching, "Yes, I'm taking
bereavement leave." He brushed a tear from under his glasses, as he
spoke to the school district. "You'll just have to find a sub."

There we were, gathered together, clustered around the bed my
grandmother's grandfather had made generations before I existed.
This is it, I thought, watching my great-aunt reach out a hand and
stroke her sister's foot. My grandma is dying. The woman who taught

me to make the perfect loaf of bread, who has read every *New Yorker* since the 1960s, who wrote poems about me as an icky adolescent, who was friends with Anaïs Nin—my grandma was at the very end of her life, her heart failing.

Later that evening, the spring light lingering on the rosebushes in the yard, I helped to fluff my grandmother's pillow and smooth her bed sheets, and thought of all the times she must have tended to my needs as a baby. We took turns through the night staying up with Grandma, and my shift began at midnight. I found a creased, worn copy of *The Witch of Blackbird Pond* and opened it, smoothing the first page. I took a breath, and began reading aloud to my grandmother, who made not a sound and moved not at all, except for the shallow rise and fall of her chest throughout the night.

Sometimes I stopped and cried a little, afraid that she might die on my watch, knowing that the end was coming soon, no matter what I read to her, no matter how many loving hands caressed her, no matter how many people told her they loved her, wished her well, released her.

At dawn, the southern California sun streamed into the living room, but the bed where my grandma lay was still deep in shadow. When the hospice nurse arrived, she felt my grandma's pulse, looked her over, and rifled through a file folder. Then, brows pinched, she picked up a bottle from the nightstand and asked, "What's this medication?"

My aunt conferred with the nurse, and in a few minutes, they were on the phone to the hospital, a doctor, and then another specialist. "They don't think its heart failure," my aunt whispered to me, cupping her hand over the phone receiver, her eyes wide. "It looks like she had a reaction to a combination of medicines."

We stared at each other, and I reached out and took my uncle's hand. Then he took my mom's hand, and she held my cousin's. And pretty soon the feeling of hope that traveled around the room was like an electric current, filling us with power, zapping us with energy.

An ambulance arrived, and my grandma was taken to the hospital. Those of us who remained at her house began chattering about something other than funerals and remembrances. "How is your husband's new job?" a family member asked me. "Did your audition go well?" I asked a cousin. Someone made soup. A neighbor came by with a fresh bouquet of roses. The phone started ringing, and as the news spread that my grandma might not be finished, the atmosphere grew lighter.

My cousin played the piano, and we all joined in song, our voices raised, weaving in and out of a melody that felt like a prayer of gratitude.

Once the doctors realized Grandma was reacting to a bad combination of medications, she recovered quickly. I went to visit her a few weeks after her experience.

"It was so scary, Grandma," I said, stroking her age-spotted hand. "I really thought you were going to go." I told her about reading to her through the night, and about the things people said to her as they took their turns saying goodbye.

"Honey," she said, "I thought so, too. And you know what? There was a kind of energy in that room, a sort of blessing swimming all around me. Even though I wasn't really awake, I felt it," she said. I was surprised to hear her words. My grandmother isn't a religious person, and she goes to a Quaker church only because of its connection to the political activism she's been committed to her whole life. "I tell you, it was amazing. All of you here, all those prayers and good feelings, I do believe that's what saved me," she said, and we both cried.

A few days later, in my own home, I lay in my bed next to my softly snoring husband, staring into the darkness, with a strange feeling in my body. The next morning was Mother's Day, and I took a pregnancy test.

Eight months later, my grandma traveled all the way from Southern California to be with me. She stood at my bedside in the hospital, reading to me between contractions. When my son was born, she was one of the first to hold him.

"Look at him," she said, her face radiant, "it really is a miracle."

And when I looked at those two beautiful faces before me—my tiny son and my grandmother—I saw two miracles.ᘒ

The Town of
Glendora, California

Population: 55,000

Town Facts

Incorporation • 1911

Location • The town of Glendora sits comfortably at the base of the San Gabriel Mountains, in the eastern portion of Los Angeles County. Glendora is approximately 20 miles east of the town of Pasadena and 30 miles northeast of downtown Los Angeles.

Origins of the town's name • Several developers joined George D. Whitcomb in 1886 and formed the Glendora Land Company. Using the last portion of George's wife's name, "Leadora," and the word "glen" (as in "mountain glen") the developers created a beautiful name for a beautiful place.

Industry • In the beginning, Glendora took advantage of the agricultural market and a perfect growing season. A variety of citrus was grown—Valencias, navels, and lemons—and industry prospered. During the Taft administration, the Glendora Mutual Orange Association became the exclusive supplier of oranges to the White House. Unfortunately, as is the case in many growing areas, urban sprawl crept across the state of California, invading the Glendora area, and soon some of the best growing soil had been surrendered to residential communities.

Famous People

Singer sewing machine heir Arthur K. Bourne built three homes in Glendora in the 1920s and 1930s. World-famous burlesque dancer and originator of the Fan Dance, Sally Rand was a long-time resident until her death in 1979. Sharon Stouder won three gold medals and one silver medal in the 1964 Tokyo Olympics as a fifteen-year-old junior from Glendora High School. She now resides with her family in northern California. Soleil Moon Frye jumped into the role of an orphan with moxie and awed her audience in the popular 1980s television series *Punky Brewster.* ❧

Flowering Landmark

The Glendora Bougainvillea, located three blocks from the civic center, is the largest growth of this subtropical vine in the continental United States. According to Galen Pittman, granddaughter to Dr. Lloyd J. Pittman, who planted the vine in 1901, twenty-three of the original twenty-eight vines still stand, some growing to an amazing proportion of thirty feet tall and twelve to fifteen feet wide. The bougainvillea is supported on a custom-made circular steel trellis that surrounds each of the 100-foot-tall Mexican fan palms, and it has been used as a postcard advertisement to draw Easterners to California. The site was also used by RKO Pictures on their newsreels in the 1930s. The photo was added to the silver screen with the phrase "Come to California" scrawled across it. Currently, the site is a California Historical Landmark (number 912), and it is also listed on the National Register of Historic Places.

Additionally, forty-six of the original orange trees planted in 1901 remain on a portion of the Glendora Bougainvillea property, which, according to available research, have been deemed the largest stand of original orange trees in existence in Los Angeles County. ❧

Transplants Who Became Townsfolk

Suzanne LaFetra writes, "My grandparents were Indiana farmers through and through, and they moved to Southern California after the war. My grandpa sold Hog Chow and Chicken Chow and all the other kinds of feed that Purina made, while my grandmother wrote poetry and raised their four children. She still lives in the same yellow house on a quiet street in Glendora, and even at ninety-two, her desk is piled high with *The New Yorker*, the *L.A. Times*, and books of poetry." ❧

In Search of a Christmas Tree

by Susan G. Sharp-Anderson | *Newport, Oregon*

WE CLIMBED OUT OF THE CAR, all bundled in our down jackets. My husband, Ray, stopped long enough to sling the saw over his shoulder before we moved into the forest. Twigs and downed branches impeded our way, but our two boys, Eric and Marcotte, aged eleven and six, sped through the underbrush like deer. I stepped slowly on the path, holding the small hand of our three-year-old daughter, Elisabeth. Thus the 1981 adventure of our annual search for a Christmas tree was initiated.

Each year, with a $2.00 permit from the National Forest Office, we trekked through the woods, the ingredients for hot chocolate and churros set out and waiting for our return in the kitchen at home. These were the requirements for cutting in the forest and decorating at the house. The children would sometimes complain about having to go out into the cold, but they were always proud of the one tree they chose, perfect in their eyes.

The particular day when we first began the tradition was cloudy, not unusual in Oregon, but there was crispness in the air, which smelled of snow. The uncertainty about snowfall made the quest more exciting.

The tradition continued each year, and each year, we thought it would be easy to pick a tree, but it never was. We'd find a beautiful little fir, and then decide that it wasn't big enough. We'd see another, and then decide that it was too big. Many times Ray agreed with one child that he had found the perfect tree, and then the other would squeal. "No, over here! Here's a better one!"

There were always so many trees that it was hard to decide upon one. And growing in the wild, they often had strange shapes. We'd think that the tree looked great, but then the backside would be flat with no significant branches.

Eventually, we would all agree on one, sometimes because we were so cold that we just wanted to go home and sometimes because it truly was the nicest tree we'd seen. Ray would saw off the trunk at ground level, occasionally assisted by Eric or Marcotte. With cheers, we watched it fall. Then the boys scrambled to drag it to the car. Ray would grab the base, while the boys took posts at the middle and the "star end."

Tying the tree to the roof of the car has always been a challenge, and that was definitely the case on this, the first time we ever attempted it. But, with blankets, ropes, and the orange permit tied to a branch, we finally made our way back through the forest to the main road, which would lead us home. It was a cold but fun romp through the woods, and we were happy to warm our fingers on the car heater with the promise of hot chocolate and pastry when we arrived home again.

At the house, we put the tree into the tree stand and immediately watered it. None of us wanted our hard work to dry out. While I started preparing the refreshments, Ray helped Eric string the lights. This job took organization and skill to make sure that they included every branch. Elisabeth picked out ornaments and handed them to Marcotte, although she occasionally wanted to hang the ornaments herself. The cat watched sleepily from the corner of the hearth, knowing that when everyone was in bed, he could play with the lower items without reprimand.

We always invited our neighbors, the Beals, to come over to share our hot food and drink, as well as to see the handiwork of nature and children. Bree and Erin, who were Marcotte's and Elisabeth's age, played happily with our children, while the adults shared their latest stories in front of the fire and newly decorated tree.

As we sat around the first tree in 1981, we were in high spirits. When the hot chocolate was ready and the churros—fluted tubes of pastry sprinkled with powdered sugar—were draining on paper towels, I set up a tray and took our treats into the living room. Everyone paused what they were doing to enjoy the companionship and sweetness of the snack.

Every year since that first snowy trek in 1981, we have annually made the sojourn. The family continues to grow, but the tradition remains the same.◡

The Visit

by Jan Sparkman | *Laurel County, Kentucky*

WHEN I RECEIVED MY GRANDDAUGHTER'S LETTER, I smiled from ear to ear. Then I sat right down and began composing a return letter.

Dear Anna,

How glad I was to hear from you! I'm guessing that not many teenage granddaughters are into actual letter writing these days.

It made my head swell to think that you're interested in how it was when I was a child. The 1950s must seem like the Dark Ages to you, but I remember so many happy times from that era.

One fall, when my family lived at what we called the "holler place" (we were always moving) Dad's cousin from Oklahoma came to visit. Our house was five miles out of town. It wasn't very big, and it had no electricity or running water. (I can just hear you saying, "Dang! That's ghetto!") Anyway, Pearl—the cousin—had not seen my dad for forty years, though they had kept in touch by mail. When Dad ended his letters by saying, "Come see us," I'm sure he had no more idea that she would actually come than she had intention of coming. Though she always answered, "One of these days I'll get back to Kentucky."

That fall, however, Pearl had a new car, and she decided to try it out by making good on her promise to visit us.

We were not expecting her. She rode into town, asked directions to our house, and showed up just in time for supper. Mama must have been ticked, to say the least. She did not have a forty-year relationship with this woman—even by mail—but she rose to the occasion, with her usual resourcefulness, and soon prepared a good meal. The details of where we all slept are fuzzy with time, but knowing my mother, I'm sure the guest had the best bed and the newest handmade quilt.

Early the next morning, Pearl gathered us children around her. "What would you like to do today?" she asked. We were silent, waiting. Gradually it dawned on us that she was saying we really could choose anything we wanted. Well, of course, we wanted to go to town. What else was there? Even in that pre-mall era it was fun to shop.

That was fine with Pearl. She loaded me and my two older sisters into her pristine Dodge and off we went. In town, she bought us new clothes, took us to a restaurant for lunch, and then asked, "What else would you like to do?"

I know you can't imagine this, but back then movies were frowned on by religious families like ours. We were told they were works of the devil—and, besides, they cost money, which we didn't have. However, since no one had told me specifically why movies were bad, I saw no reason not to go to one while I had the chance. When I announced this in response to Pearl's question, my sisters gasped. They pinched me and whispered that Dad would kill us, but Pearl was already asking the way to the theater and before we knew it, there we were, watching cowboys and Indians ride wildly across the big screen. It was a defining experience in my young life and no amount of concern about my father's displeasure could keep me from enjoying it. I don't even remember being swallowed up by guilt afterward.

It was as if Pearl's visit had suspended our real life. We had already decided that Pearl was rich, so when she remarked, as we watched a seemingly endless herd of cattle tramp over a dusty prairie, "I have three times that many cows on my ranch in Oklahoma," we did not suspect her of being ostentatious. As it turned out, she wasn't boasting. She had married a real-life cattle baron at a time when cattle were the lifeblood of the Oklahoma plains, and together they ran a large ranch. What she spent on us that day was nothing compared to what she could have spent if she had been so inclined. At any rate, she did not need to make a point of her wealth to us. We were already as impressed as it was possible to be.

For a few hours, Cousin Pearl gave us a glimpse of a larger world and our delight was boundless. Furthermore, the confidence of her manner convinced us she could handle any problems our disobedience might cause with our parents. Sure enough, with Pearl running interference, we sailed right through Dad's objections to the movie and Mama's questions about whether or not we had rudely begged Pearl for the things she bought us. We were glad we could say we hadn't asked for anything (except the movie) so Mama wouldn't have to be ashamed of us.

That was the first and last time Pearl ever visited us, but I've never forgotten her. And I still remember how elegant I felt in my new dress. It was bright green with a pocket in the shape of a flower.

Love, and keep writing me,
Grandma Jan

As I put the letter in the mail, I pictured Anna's smiling face, and my heart skipped a beat in anticipation of our next correspondence.

The Bunny of Easters Past

by Jean Davidson | *Providence, Utah*

I REACHED UP AND TUGGED GENTLY ON THE STRING, letting light into the dark and musty room. There, against the far wall, under a velvet-smooth layer of dust, was the cedar chest—just as I remembered it. I carefully brushed away the dust and lifted the lid of the old blonde chest. The pungent smell of cedar immediately wafted up into my nostrils, and timeless memories came swarming. There, inside the chest, lying on top and carefully wrapped in time-yellowed sheets of tissue, was the bunny—the bunny of Easters past.

With near reverence, I pulled away the wrappings and checked him over. I smiled. Although a little worse for wear, the still-bright pinks and blues of his painted-on coat were visible among the missing chips of paint. The tip of one of his long, dished-in ears was slightly crushed, and his papier-mâché body bore witness to lots of touching. This was a hazard of his occupation, for sure. I closed my eyes and went back there again, back to the bunny hunt at Grandpa's house on Easter Sunday 1948.

Each year our extended families made the pilgrimage to Providence, Utah, to help celebrate Grandpa's birthday. On some lucky occasions, the birthday fell close to Easter so we enjoyed a double celebration. After a lavish German feast of baked goose, red cabbage, *kuchen,* and other sumptuous foods, the excitement of the pending egg hunt would begin to grow. All of us children, ranging in ages from three to sixteen, were confined in the kitchen, with the older kids guarding the doors and windows so none of us could escape or see outside. They teased us with warnings to watch out for foxes, which stalked little Easter bunnies, and to watch out for hawks. In the distance, doors mysteriously opened and closed, and then we heard someone call out, "I think I see him."

Squeals of excitement erupted from our group. We squirmed and giggled and fidgeted all about, consumed with the heightening thrill and fever of a chase about to begin.

"He's out there—I see him," someone else hollered from somewhere distant, but still we were kept imprisoned in the kitchen. More doors opened and closed. More voices called out. Then we heard Grandpa coming.

Grandpa was a large man, rotund and bald, with an infectious grin and a warm, loving personality. Laughter often rumbled out of him from deep within, like an oncoming locomotive, infecting everyone in the vicinity. Still, when he entered a room, there was instant respect and proper behavior.

"We must find the rabbit," he announced somberly, his eyes twinkling. "And we must gather the eggs. Who will help?"

"We will, we will," everyone cheered. His face beamed with delight.

"Does everyone have baskets?"

Everyone shouted at once. "Yes, yes! We have baskets!"

"There's a chocolate prize for whoever catches the bunny," he reminded us. Then he turned to the door, signaling the hunt was about to begin. A dozen steps later, we were crowding through the glass French doors headed out of the house. Our feet hit the yard running. We were free at last to begin the hunt.

Behind the house and on both sides were pastures, lush with tall, green grass and edged with apple trees. Along one side of the house grew Grandma's treasured raspberry bushes. It was always my suspicion that the bunny especially liked hiding in there. But when it came to the small irrigation stream edging the property out by the street, I was nervous for the bunny. I was never sure he could leap that ditch.

Still, it was a wonderful neighborhood for an Easter bunny to hide his treasures in, and I relished scrapping and fighting for every egg I could see.

The hunt was thrilling. It truly left no stone unturned. Just about the time our little baskets were filled with eggs, someone called from the porch. "He made it inside. The bunny's inside! Hurry, hurry!"

Pushing and shoving, we scrambled through the doors to assault the hiding places within the house itself. We checked everything: the basement, the closets, the cupboards, and the pantry. One of the kids even peered cautiously down the laundry chute, trying to decide if the bunny was daring enough to make that harrowing one-way trip into the basement. Suddenly, we heard a shout of success. "I have it, I have it!"

One of the older children sauntered proudly into the living room, the ever-smiling papier-mâché bunny in one hand, a chocolate, foil-covered bunny in the other.

Needless to say, we were all green with envy. But, we were pleased, too. We had collectively met the challenge and successfully captured the bunny—again. Life was wonderful.

The bunny disappeared later that day but showed up again the following year, ready for another run-of-the-bunny.

Half a dozen years later, our grandparents were gone from us, so the bunny was quietly retired into Grandma's old cedar chest for a well-earned rest.

Now, fifty years later, he's coming to live at my house. With my grandkids' help, his adventures will begin again. And so will mine. ❧

Scents of Remembrance

by Avis A. Townsend | *Lockport, New York*

ALTHOUGH SHE'S BEEN GONE FOR FIFTY YEARS, I still remember Grandma—her squeaky voice, the funny laugh she had, and the sound of her footsteps as she clomped along in her black lace-up shoes.

In her final years, Grandma spent each weekend in our home. She was deaf and wore a hearing aid, so the best way to wake her was by tickling her chin.

Each morning, she'd comb and coil her long white hair. I was fascinated by that ritual. Uncoiled, her hair reached the floor. She brushed it until it shone like silk, and then she'd take it up in handfuls and started winding, around and around. She'd anchor the coil with just one hairpin; then she'd grab another handful and start all over, until all the coils were pinned neatly on top of her head. And they'd stay that way, even in the strongest wind.

I was ten years old when Grandma left this earth. My mother said she died with a smile on her face, "as if she knew." But if she knew, I reasoned, why would she smile about it? You don't smile when you're about to die, do you? I was crushed.

For Grandma's viewing, I went to the funeral home twice each day. Suffering through each visitation, I listened to relatives talk about her and say she would have loved the many baskets of flowers. I hated the flowers. They represented her death, and somehow that made them ugly. People filing past her casket remarked about how well she looked, but I thought she looked different.

I was devastated. I sat motionless on a stiff chair directly across from the casket, staring at my beloved Grandma's face, heartbroken that I would never hear her voice again. My mother realized it wasn't healthy for me to be sitting there like that, so she asked my cousin, Joanne, to take me for a ride. Joanne had just bought a used 1950 Chevy. She was eighteen, and as she drove she sang aloud to the music on the radio. Within minutes we had arrived at Outwater Park. The park sat high on a hill above Glenwood Avenue, the road where my grandmother had lived most of her adult life. It was also the road to Glenwood Cemetery.

We had a pleasant time at the park, and it did take my mind off my sorrow for a little while. There were interesting stone steps at the north end of the park, and we followed them down the hill to Glenwood Avenue. In various places along the path, where rays of sunshine had peeked through tree branches, clumps of wild violets grew freely. I stopped to take a deep breath, enjoying their sweet fragrance immensely. The scent was familiar and made me feel secure, but I couldn't figure out why. Eventually, I stopped and picked a small clump, holding the flowers to my nose and sniffing their aroma as we walked along.

Joanne smiled. "Those were Grandma's favorite flowers. Did you know that? They grew wild on her property. She'd cut them and put them in vases all over her house."

Of course! Grandma's house had the same sweet smell as the flowers I held in my hand. I sniffed again, thinking of Grandma and how much I missed her, and blinked back tears.

Joanne put her hand on my shoulder. "Grandma wouldn't want you to be sad. She lived a long life. She'd want you to be happy about that."

"I know," I said, "but I didn't get to know her long enough. You're older. I'm just a kid."

At the bottom of the hill, we spotted the entrance to Glenwood Cemetery. I stopped and turned to Joanne.

"Is this where she's going to be?"

"It's where we'll all be, eventually," Joanne said. "We have a family plot. Do you want to see it?"

"No," I said at first. But then I changed my mind.

When we walked through the gates of the cemetery, we stopped, awed at the sight in front of us. The grounds were dotted with purple—wild violets grew everywhere!

"I don't remember seeing so many of them here before," Joanne said. She seemed more in awe than I was. "It's like they're welcoming Grandma here."

As we walked to the family plot the fragrance of violets filled the air. Everywhere we looked, purple clumps crowded out the grass, and in that instant I felt Grandma was with us.

Before we left, I grabbed another bunch of violets and tucked them inside the cuff of my sock. When I returned to the funeral home, after all the guests had left, I walked up to my grandmother and put the petals on her pillow, hiding them under the pink rose bouquet that said "Grandma," so no one could take them away. They were her favorite flower, yet no one had brought any for her.

I now live in an old farmhouse on fifty acres. Each spring, daffodils bloom and tulips peek happily over long green stems and puff adders and trilliums dot the woodlands. It's a beautiful sight to behold. But nothing thrills me as much as the clumps of wild violets growing freely across the yard.

My mother's wisdom eased my grieving. If Joanne hadn't taken me to the park that day, I might have lost Grandma forever.

Watermelon Preserves

by Margaret Anne Wright | *Purdin, Missouri*

HAVING BEEN BORN AND RAISED IN ONTARIO, CANADA, I never understood why my grade school teachers told me that I talked with a slight accent. I never dreamed that my accent originated from Missouri. But on this hot humid afternoon, as I stopped the small rental car in front of the Purdin Mercantile—a red-brick hardware store in Missouri with a diamond-shaped sign—I realized that this was where it had all begun. The store looked as if it had been there since my mother was a child in the 1920s.

I turned to my mother and smiled. I was glad to have the opportunity to take her to Missouri for the family reunion. She was enjoying herself, and I was gaining a sense of personal history.

Walking across the wide main street toward an old whitewashed community hall, I noticed my mother smile when she recognized an elderly lady in a blue-and-white pantsuit.

"Audrey!" Ma said, embracing the other woman.

I soon learned that Audrey was Ma's first cousin, as were Minnie, Pearl, Nelson, and Willie. Although it was hard to remember everyone's name, being around relatives gave me a sense of identity—an identity I didn't know I had.

Entering the busy hall, I noticed that old wooden chairs had been placed around long tables with red-checked tablecloths. In the corner of the room was a kitchen where many ladies were preparing a buffet luncheon. With the exception of the American flag, I felt like I could have been at a church gathering in Ontario.

Across the room, I recognized my Uncle Malcolm and his family from Saskatchewan. When I shyly smiled at them, Aunt Jolene walked over and gave me a big hug. Slowly, the rest of her family joined us. It had been fifteen years since I'd seen some of them, but we quickly became reacquainted.

After twenty minutes of chatting, my cousins' attention was diverted to other relatives. I eyed my mother talking with an older gentleman and moved toward them. The man quickly introduced himself as another second cousin. We chatted for a few minutes before someone summoned him for a group photograph.

"Whose picture do you want me to take?" I asked my mother, remembering that I was the designated family photographer.

"Take a picture of those two guys," she said.

I quickly flashed a picture of the two old men—one of the men being my Uncle Malcolm.

"Who is the man with Uncle Malcolm?" I asked.

"Fergus Gunter," my mother replied. She wore an impish grin on her face, and I knew that there was a humorous story surrounding the association of these two men.

"What does Fergus Gunter have in common with Uncle Malcolm?"

"They were both watermelon thieves," she blurted, a giggle bubbling up her throat.

"Were they charged?" I asked.

"Back in the 1920s kids weren't charged the way they are today," Ma explained. "Parents usually dealt with their own wayward kids."

"It sounds like parents encouraged stealing."

"No, these kids were just having fun. One kid would take a watermelon one night and the next night the other kid would take it back again. It was more of a neighborhood game than stealing." I had often wondered what people did for entertainment before television—now I knew.

Looking at Uncle Malcolm and Fergus Gunter patting each other on the back, I realized that neighbors in the 1920s had been close. There was community. In my own neighborhood, I only knew one person in my apartment building. I listened intently as Ma continued with her story.

"One night Malcolm and Fergus came to our house in their underwear, their overalls slung over their backs. They were excited about their latest conquest—widow Caldwell's watermelon patch. By taking off their overalls and tying a knot in each of the pant legs, Malcolm and Fergus were able to take sixteen watermelons at the same time. That's when your grandma ended the watermelon snatching."

"What did she do?"

"She made the boys take the watermelons into the pantry, where they were cut open and scooped clean. Your grandma then made watermelon preserves. For the next year, Malcolm and Fergus were often seen taking a jar of watermelon preserves to Mrs. Caldwell. Occasionally, your grandma and I visited Mrs. Caldwell. She never knew who had taken her watermelons that night and she just knew it couldn't be nice boys like Malcolm and Fergus."

A Few Minutes Ago

by Kristine Ziemnik | *Chippewa Lake, Ohio*

WHAT COMES TO MIND FIRST, when I think about that evening, is how beautiful the night was. My daughter, Andrea, and I had just arrived at the historic Ohio Theater, in Playhouse Square, downtown Cleveland. We were both awed by the coffered ceilings and the beautiful art glass oval insets scattered throughout the building. The air was filled with joyful chatter as the audience waited for the show to begin.

We were seeing the hit musical, *Mamma Mia!*, which is based on the songs of the recording group ABBA. Andrea knew I loved theatrical productions, especially musicals, and had taken advantage of a good thing. This was my Mother's Day present.

While we waited for the show to begin, we made small talk about Andrea's upcoming June wedding. We were both excited as we discussed the wedding plans, and even more so when the curtain went up and we learned the story line revolved around the wedding of a young girl and her own wedding preparations.

Like most musicals, there was the usual dialogue, songs, and in this one, plenty of laughs. In one scene, the daughter sits at her dressing table on the day of the wedding and her mom starts to remember when her little girl left home on the first day of school.

I didn't realize the song would affect me so much, but before it ended I was in tears and hastily rummaging through my purse for a tissue. I could relate to how the mom was feeling. I bit my lip to keep from letting the sob in my throat escape. The theatrical wedding taking place onstage was a reminder of what would take place in a few weeks in my own life. Andrea would walk down the aisle. It seemed like only a few minutes ago that my lovely daughter had been just a little girl, holding my hand, going to school for the first time. Now she was slipping through my fingers. Soon she would be holding the hand of her new husband.

Taking a deep breath, I managed to calm down enough to enjoy the rest of the performance. Andrea glanced over and noticed my mascara was smeared across my cheeks.

"Aw, Mom," she whispered, giving me a gentle hug. "You're so sentimental."

She'd hit the nail on the head. I am sentimental, and that is not something that will ever go away. It's the deep feelings inside of me that make me who I am, and though it hurts at times, I wouldn't change it for the world.

Two years later, Andrea and I were in the same luxurious theater watching the very same musical. This time, Beth, my youngest daughter, was with us. Because Andrea and I had enjoyed the play so much, we wanted to share it with Beth.

As we watched, I realized I'd forgotten some parts. The jokes seemed funnier and the actors had more energy. The story line was proceeding along smoothly when it hit me all over again. The bedroom scene with mother and daughter was coming up.

I looked at Andrea, and then I frantically dug in my purse for tissues. Andrea had been married for two years already. Beth would be walking down the aisle in a few months, and we were once more in the midst of wedding plans. I knew the song would stir up feelings of sadness. My little girl was to become a bride, leaving the shelter of our home to make a new home with her husband.

Unexpectedly, Andrea took my hand and entwined her arm with mine. She held my hand through the whole song, leaving my other hand free to wipe away the tears. Having been through the experience once herself, she knew what I was feeling in my heart for Beth, who, I swear, had been a little girl just a few minutes ago.

Biting my lip as hard as I could—a trick I learned the last time I saw this play—I felt Andrea lean her head toward me and heard her sing along with the actress. Andrea added her own last line to the song about the little girl leaving for school and waving goodbye: "She gets stung by a bee!"

My heart lurched as memories flooded over me. That was exactly what had happened on Beth's first day of school. Though it was a long time ago, I could remember it as clearly as if it had been yesterday. As the school bus approached, a bee stung my little kindergartener. I had to put her on the bus crying. I remember asking the driver to call me if she was still upset when she got to school.

I looked at Andrea and the tears stopped in midstream. We both giggled as we thought of the incident. After the play, we let Beth in on the cause of our laughter and my tears.

"Aw, Mom," Beth teased. "You're so sentimental!"

Now, where had I heard that before?

I thought of all the songs in the play and realized that "Slipping Through My Fingers" will probably be the only one that I remember in the years to come. It's the one that will bring to mind how Andrea remembered my emotion from the first time we saw the musical together and how she held my hand while I cried the second time I saw it with both of my girls. I will recall how I reminisced about my daughters, my two beautiful daughters, who were only little girls just a few minutes ago.

Dixie Pool

by Rachael Phillips | *Eros, Louisiana*

"Aren't you gonna swim, Grandp—Pawpaw?"

The name filled my mouth like the giant buttery biscuits my grandmother baked for breakfast—not at all unpleasant, just very different. I was a young Yankee from "up north," unaccustomed to addressing grandparents as "Pawpaw" and "Mammy," the accepted titles of love and respect that came so easily to my cousins.

Pawpaw's eyes twinkled. He sat on the orange clay bank and thrust his jaw forward in a smile that reminded me of a friendly bulldog. "No, honey," he rumbled in his deep bass voice. "Ya'll swim, and I'll just watch." I looked on as sweat poured down his face. He was wearing his usual heavy gray pants and long-sleeved shirt. Dressed like that, he made me feel hot just looking at him.

I paddled away to join my siblings and cousins in the clear, cold ecstasy of Dixie Pool, a round mirror-like pond. My father's family always gathered to swim in Dixie Pool during our annual visits to Eros, a sleepy little town in the northern Louisiana pinewoods. When the summer heat and humidity lay on us all like a smothering quilt, we sat for hours on the screened-in porch while my father and his sisters told endless stories from their childhood, or we headed for Dixie Pool. It goes without saying which I liked best.

My father and uncles yelled and swung across the spring on a rope, like Tarzan. My older brother did cannonballs off the bank and walked on his hands underwater. My cousins and I played motorboat with the little ones, whirling them around in circles until we all fell down amidst a chorus of laughter, cries, and gurgles, sinking below the surface only to come up sputtering and spewing water.

Our mothers, wading at the spring's edge like pretty herons, objected to our drowning our younger siblings, so we left the toddlers on their own and played a different game, called "tea and crackers."

Tea and crackers was an underwater game. We each sat on the bottom of the pool, tipping imaginary teapots into our pretend cups, eating from invisible plates, and wiping our lips daintily before rising to the surface. We swam races—which I always lost—and dove for the smooth red pebbles we treasured as if they were rubies. Sometimes we clung to round watermelons from Pawpaw's patch as we swam. They kept us afloat and later doubled as a sweet, chilly snack.

I liked Dixie Pool better than any lake at home. The bottom was firm, as if it had been designed for our swimming party, not squishy and obscene with mysterious goo and unnamed life forms.

All the while we swam and played, Pawpaw sat alone, his worn, leathery hands folded, watching us frolic as if we were a bunch of dolphins on the vast ocean. Occasionally, he donned his gold-rimmed glasses to read from a plain little black book. As I swam away from Pawpaw after inviting him to join us, I decided then and there never to get old. Old people never had any fun.

Flipping over onto my back, I attempted to float as my swimming instructor, Miss Angie, had taught me. Suddenly, a huge *WHUMPF* sounded behind me and a wave of cold water swept over my face. I dropped to the bottom like a rock. Choking and sputtering, I crawled to my feet, poised to bawl like an indignant calf. If I cried loud enough, surely my brother would suffer dire consequences for doing a cannonball too close.

But when the waters parted, it was Pawpaw who emerged from Dixie Pool, water streaming from his hair, his face shining, his eyes sparkling with triumph! Fully dressed, he had flipped off the bank in a dive that they say had surpassed the best show-off in the group. Pawpaw's adult children stood speechless, jaws slack with disbelief. The grandchildren slapped their wet hands together like baby seals and shouted their adulation. Within twenty-four hours, all of Eros knew their town patriarch, the devout biblical scholar with the sixth-grade education, had scored a perfect ten, guaranteed to have put Olympic-caliber dives to shame.

Forty-five years later, I remember Pawpaw and Dixie Pool, and leave my safe, comfortable spot on the bank to do a few flips of my own.໑

THE TOWN OF
Eros, Louisiana
Population: 202

Town Facts

Incorporation • The town was founded in 1898 by the Tremont Lumber Company.

Location • It is situated in Jackson Parish.

Origins of the town's name • The Greek word *eros* means love, and, as local residents tell the story, Pearl Collins was in fact thinking about her love for astronomy when she suggested the town be named Eros, in honor of an asteroid German astronomer Dr. G. Witt had discovered in 1898.

Famous names • A well-known bluegrass songwriter and musician, the now deceased Buzz Busby (Bernarr Graham Busbice), was born in Eros.

Town History

The post office plays a significant part in Eros's history. It was one of the first businesses to set up shop, and though it has been uprooted and relocated three times, it still survives today. It is also noted as being the only building that was covered by insurance when a tornado struck in 1920, destroying the town.

In 1911, a small town fire destroyed part of the Tremont Lumber Company mill, but the company knew a good thing when they saw it. Rather than close up shop, they opted to enlarge and expand, turning their mill into the largest in northern Louisiana.

By 1920, Eros, the biggest town in the parish, had such amenities as two hotels, three churches and three doctors, a high school, and its own telephone exchange. Unfortunately, the town was destroyed that year when a tornado struck. The tornado spared the lives of the townsfolk, but it took everything else in its path. Within minutes, a town that had stood proudly for thirty years had been leveled. But Eros was rebuilt, the mill was re-opened, and life went on as usual. In 1926, however, a second fire destroyed the mill, and the boom town faded into obscurity. ∽

Historians Speak about Olden Days

*L*urline Phillip (eighty-four years of age) and Svea Freeland (age seventy-four) recall Eros in its early days as a rough town with dirt streets, where cattle roamed freely and Sheriff Gunner was killed attempting to uphold the law. They note that Miss Leila Harper's general store was "the" gathering place. The building, now Bill's Country Store, still remains, and a vault from the original bank sits near a basketball court, providing shade to youngsters from the hot Louisiana sun.

Today, city improvements continue to be the main focus, and, aside from a lack of city sewers, Eros is as up-to-date as any small town can hope to be. ∽

The Oglesbees of Eros

*A*ctive in their community, the Oglesbees at one time filled the "O" section of the small telephone directory in Eros, Louisiana. One of Fillmore "Pawpaw" Oglesbee's daughters, Lurlina, was married to the mayor, Dee Phillips. But today, most of the Eros Oglesbee family and their descendants have scattered . Both young and old, gather to recap old times and catch up on new at the 100-year-old house in the pine woods near Eros, where Pawpaw and Mammie Oglesbee once lived. Their daughter, Svea Freeland, now welcomes the long-lost with "Ya'll come in!" After a round of hugs worthy of Pawpaw's powerful embrace, Eros relatives regale travelers with a southern banquet including Mammie's white coconut cake, sweet and rich and pure as love. Afterward, everyone enjoys storytelling on the screened-in porch, as in years gone by—including family tales like "Dixie Pool." ∽

My Chair

Penny Porter | *Esopus, New York*

I HAD MY VERY OWN STRAIGHT-BACKED CHAIR at my great-grandfather's dining room table. It was identical to the other eleven, with fine-tooled, mahogany rungs crisscrossing at various levels under the seat, and it offered a silent invitation for my endlessly long legs and restless feet to explore. My chair had an identity of its own: It was perfectly matched with the others, except that one of the shiny upholstery tacks, which held the smooth leather seat in place, was missing.

As if I were translating Braille, I walked my fingers along those cool brass tack heads, counting, rooting through the gap left by the departed one, until the sum total assured me there were exactly thirty-one. Only then did I know for sure this was *my* chair—the one with the loose spire that never could withstand the power of a nervous twist when it was my turn to stand behind the chair and address the eleven expectant faces around the banquet-size table.

My Aunt Mary and Uncle Ted lived in Great-Grandfather's home then, their hearts ever open to my younger brother, Parker, and me—provided we were accompanied by a governess. Abandoned by our parents, we spent several weeks in this house each summer, and an occasional Christmas. Although they had three children of their own, my aunt and uncle opened their home in Esopus, New York, to other youngsters, and filled empty rooms during the Depression years. There we learned about love and life, and the world, from mahogany chairs.

A favorite family custom passed down through the years from our great-grandfather, Alton Brooks Parker, took place during Friday dinner. Known as "Baypa" to all who loved him, this great appeals-court judge had lost to Theodore Roosevelt in the presidential election of 1904, but that didn't stop him from continually reaching forward to better himself and those around him. "Not a day should pass," Baypa said, "that we not learn something new and pass it on to family and friends." So it was that on Friday evenings that every child and guest at the table was asked to stand behind his or her chair and share a learning experience that would be of value to all present.

The year I turned eleven is seated firmly in my soul. I had grown twelve inches in the eleven months since my cousins and friends had last seen me. I had been taxied to every doctor in New York City for answers. At nearly six feet tall and just seventy-nine pounds, my size was reason enough to keep me out of sight as much as possible. Adults whispered. Children pointed. I did not look like the child locked inside my body. A future with Barnum and Bailey often crossed my mind. I stammered and was unconquerably shy; I prayed to be forgiven the terrifying act of speaking.

The meal over, my teeth chattered as Uncle Ted addressed the black-robed Episcopal bishop seated to his right. "I think you will enjoy this part of our Friday night program, Bishop," he said. "The youngest child will be called upon first. If he is unable to speak long enough to fill five minutes with a learning experience, questions and discussion are allowed. We will take turns around the table." This meant I would be last.

My cousins, musically gifted, spoke easily on something new they had learned about Beethoven, Bach, Brahms, or Tchaikovsky. My brother, an athlete from age three, told about great golfers of the year such as Sammy Snead and Byron Nelson, while the other four children, all avid readers, shared stories of President Roosevelt, the burning of the *Hindenburg,* Babe Ruth of baseball fame, and a lame racehorse named Seabiscuit. Neither musical, athletic, nor a reader, my heart hammered in my chest.

"Penny." My uncle's voice seemed to echo from a well. "What will you share with us?"

Forgetting my legs and feet were hopelessly ensnared among chair rungs, I tried to get up. Over went my glass of milk, a white river that flowed relentlessly across five feet of varnished mahogany, and plunged into the bishop's lap. At last, legs free, I stood up, grabbed the spires on the back of my chair, and twisted the unglued one too hard. The spire shot backward, over my head, and struck the portrait of my great-grandfather in the nose.

"Mercy!" said Aunt Mary. That was her favorite word.

I let go of my chair, and turned to glance at Baypa's portrait. Was that dust, or a dent under the Chief Justice's nose now? What did it matter? The stern walrus mustache had softened and seemed to reveal a smile. That was all the encouragement I needed to survive the next five minutes, my turn to enchant the listeners at the family gathering with a secret that I alone knew.

"Penny!" Again, Uncle Ted's voice pulled me back to the moment.

"Well," I began, "there's this wonderful magazine called *The National Geographic.* Yesterday, I found one in Baypa's library." I paused for a minute, recalling the yellow stripe—wedged between burgundy law books—that had made it so easy to find. But why had it been relegated to the top shelf, I wondered, out of reach of children . . . except me? "I like it," I continued, "because it's full of beautiful pictures, and not so many words, pictures of islands in the

Pacific Ocean where palm trees full of coconuts grow, and pictures of ladies with flowers in their hair . . . and . . . and . . ." And in the next instant I had graphically explained that these ladies were naked from the waist up.

"Mercy!" Aunt Mary choked, pressed her napkin to her lips, as she continued mopping up my milk from the bishop's clothing.

Fifty years later, I drove back to Baypa's ancestral home, searching for the windows of light that occasionally shine through a dark child-life. I found that Baypa's portrait and pieces of furniture had been donated to the Kingston Museum nearby. But it was Sunday, and the museum was closed. Since no one was around, I walked along the attached verandah and peeked through the windows.

Hanging over a mantel in a gilded frame, Judge Parker wore the same smile that had warmed the chills of my childhood. I cupped my hands around my face to better see the artifacts beneath him—a couch, a globe, a judge's robe, and a few leather books on an occasional table. But it was the chair in the corner that caught my eye, the chair that blurred my vision. It was missing one brass tack and a spire at the top of the straight mahogany back.

My chair.

Swamp Family

by Lucile C. Cason | *Fargo, Georgia*

THE NEED TO DODGE RATTLESNAKES and the unavoidable accumulation of mosquito and tick bites are not enough to deter family and friends who gather yearly for the Shirley Family Reunion, held at the edge of Okefenokee Swamp. In fact, half-submerged alligators near muddy banks only add to the delight of the adventurous relatives who rent boats to tour historic Billy's Island, which is inland from the Stephen Foster State Park near Fargo, Georgia. The tradition of meeting at the swamp began when Grandmother's small home could no longer accommodate the family and friends who gathered to celebrate her birthday.

Things were done differently back then. Grandmother Shirley was a mere fourteen years old when she married her seventeen-year-old sweetheart and began housekeeping. Granddaddy worked in the pine forests, cutting notches into the trees to gather the gum from which turpentine and other tar products are made. As an engineer, he also ran a locomotive that pulled cypress logs from the swamp to be sawed into timber. He died before I came into the family, but I understand he knew how to make a fiddle sing, while his children and friends square-danced late into the night.

I was, however, honored to know and love Grandmother Shirley. She visited my home once a few years after I had gotten married and said she'd had "as good a meal as I've ever eaten." How good that felt to hear!

After Grandmother's death in 1980, family and friends continued meeting at the same time, at the same place. One son and four daughters, all in their eighties and nineties, remain from the original family of nine children. Sheltered picnic tables support pots of fresh fish, caught by the local fishermen and fried to perfection. Hushpuppies, grits, buckets of chicken, potato salad, casseroles, cakes, pies, and homemade ice cream are among the shared delectables. The descendents, dragging initially reluctant spouses, children, and friends, come from Florida, Georgia, and as far away as California. Warmth from the welcoming love and hospitality of family soon melts any lingering resistance. One grandson married a beautiful Vietnamese woman when he was stationed in Saigon, and now her family is part of our swamp family, too.

Cousin David brings cases of gallberry or orange honey in his pickup truck to sell to a captive audience. Gallberry bushes grow in the swamp and other parts of South Georgia and North Florida. The bitter berries make some of the best honey ever. When the orange trees are blooming in Florida, David carries his bees down to gather nectar from the ocean of white blossoms. Some prefer the hint of orange in their honey, but most locals stand by the gallberry.

Kinfolks retell favorite stories or present comedy skits, and bluegrass tunes challenge the cry of cicadas and herons when grandchildren bring out their guitars and mandolins. Those who are unaccustomed to the Southern heat slip away to tour the air-conditioned Park Museum, and learn about swamp wildlife and vegetation. Others rent canoes or boats at the park store to see if the fish are biting or to tour the waterways.

On one trip, I joined family and friends who rented jonboats. We went to Billy's Island to see the rusting relics of train engines and tracks remaining from the 1930s, when the island was inhabited by turpentine workers and farmers and timber harvesting thrived. I loved seeing the long-legged swamp birds that fish knee-deep in the dark water, equally alert for signs of food or danger. At the narrow dock on Billy's Island I climbed off first. I noticed how the dock barely cleared the dark water. Floating pine needles and dead leaves made it hard to see where planks ended and water began. Uriah, my son Bart's friend, was next. This was his first trip into the swamp. He took the rope Bart tossed him and stepped back to secure the boat. One moment I was watching him—the next moment he had disappeared.

"Uriah?"

His head bobbed among the pine needles and leaves, his chin level with the dock. A brief expletive bubbled from his lips along with a mouthful of swamp water.

Instead of helping him, my son bent over in laughter, nearly capsizing the boat. My motherly concern surfaced and I gasped, "Uriah, there are alligators in there!"

Instantly, he heaved himself up onto the dock and stood drip-drying.

The word Okefenokee hails from a Native American word for "trembling earth." A trembling Uriah couldn't decide whether to be angry at Bart and me for laughing or to be grateful he hadn't been gator bait. Reluctantly, he joined us in laughter. By the time we had marveled at how the swamp had reclaimed an area where more than 400 people once lived and worked, Uriah's clothing was dry and his name was on everyone's lips. Unbeknownst to Uriah, he was destined for fame. His story is now one of the favorites heard recited over and over again among his Cason friends during the Shirley Family Reunions in Okefenokee Swamp.

Every spring, just as the birds from the northern states and Canada flock to the Okefenokee swamp for winter, the divergent branches of the Shirley family descendants and friends return to their roots. Here they cherish the nourishment of belonging to a part of history. ❧

Getting Up with the Sun

by Kimberly Zweygardt | *Protection, Kansas*

EVERY MORNING OF MY CHILDHOOD, Daddy drove to my grand-parents' farm to feed the cattle. Though only 13 miles from town, it seemed exotically far away from my house in the little Kansas town I grew up in, and I loved to ride along. Part of my bedtime ritual was begging Daddy to let me go with him in the morning.

"You'll have to get up early," Daddy would caution. But I didn't care. Going to the farm with Daddy was small price to pay for getting up with the sun.

The next morning, as the moon faded into the azure sky and the red sun peeped over the flat horizon, Daddy tucked me into the seat of his old pickup truck, bundled like a mummy in my blue coat. Before his first cup of steaming coffee, he'd cranked the engine, the blowing heat turning the cab into an island of warmth, musty with the faint smell of manure.

The whole way, Daddy sang songs such as "The Blue Yodel" and "Mama and Papa Waltz," his tenor soaring over the growl of the engine as we headed south on the gravel road, past the fencepost sentinels guarding the short-grass pastures and fields that were white with frost. To my four-year-old mind it seemed like a long journey, but I was content in the warmth of the truck cab listening to Daddy sing.

Ascending into Pleasant Valley, I'd begin the refrain, "I see Grandma's House! I see Grandma's house!" Bright green winter wheat fields lay before us—the shade of leprechauns' coats, the small farm and outbuildings spreading across the waistline. A shelter of elm trees, planted during the Depression and gnarled by the Kansas wind, guarded the little house from the road, shadowing the lane.

From seven children and countless grandchildren that had swung round its posts, the gingerbread porch looked like a white party dress that had lost its starch. Grandma's rock collection lined the walk, the pink quartz glinting in the morning sun. Rex, the farm dog, barked a greeting and scattered the chickens that were busy scratching out a meal of bugs in the sparse brown grass near the house. Hereford cattle bawled hungrily from their pens, appetites whetted by the pungent tang of silage on the morning air and the sight of Daddy's truck.

Daddy joined Granddad and Uncle John at the silo and I waved goodbye as Grandma threw open the kitchen door in greeting. Grandma's kitchen was steamy and crowded. A sturdy table, dressed in red-and-white checked oilcloth, sat in the heart of the room, surrounded by a massive cook stove, an old enamel kitchen sink, a washtub where the men splashed sweat and dirt from their faces and arms before sitting at Grandma's table, and a Hoosier cabinet where Grandma kept her "receipts" for cookies and cakes and puddings. Limp red-and-white dotted Swiss curtains added a touch of color. The worn tan linoleum mapped Grandma's years of travels around the room.

Hot grease sizzled merrily as Grandma bustled about, frying hot cakes. Sweet butter floated in a sea of sorghum syrup, drenching the cakes on the Ironstone platter. The cakes were fluffy inside and crisped brown around the edges, the tangy sweet syrup a perfect complement to a glass of cold milk. Grandma's graying hair curled up around her dimpled cheeks, her soft plump hands constantly smoothing her flowered apron or my stray curls. Being hugged by Grandma was like being swept into a featherbed scented with "Evening in Paris" perfume.

With a blast of cold fall air, the men burst into the kitchen, as hungry as the cattle they had just fed, bringing with them talk of farm prices and the scent of the outdoors. The big round table overflowed with family, food, laughter, and love while Grandma beamed her delight. No one would go home hungry from her table if she had any say-so.

Much too soon, it was time to go.

On the ride home, I drifted off to sleep, nestled against Daddy's shoulder, and love and contentment colored my dreams, accompanied by the crunch of gravel and Daddy's voice as he softly crooned. ✧

The Family Together

by Sam E. Douglas | *Chester, South Carolina*

WHEN I LET MY MIND DRIFT, it invariably settles on happy times
from my youth—the occasions that revolved around family gatherings. When I was growing up in the South during the 1940s and
1950s, someone in the family was always having a birthday or graduation, going away to college or the military, getting married, or having
a baby.

Among all those happy times, the family gathering that stands
out most for me was generated from a situation that was, in fact,
not happy at all. My favorite gathering celebrated the return of me
and my sisters from the orphanage where Mom had been forced to
leave us when divorce broke up our immediate family. My siblings
and I were in the orphanage only a few months, but we found it
unbearable. The day Mother found a factory job and a small basement apartment was the happiest day of our lives. It meant we were
going home.

We gathered at my aunt's house, and it was immediately clear
that my sisters and I were the stars of the show. All the adults gathered around us and hugged us and told us how happy they were

that we were "back home." All the hoopla made us feel special, but because the occasion itself quickly became just like all those we had enjoyed over the years, the event even more special. Our lives were back to normal.

The food was the same as always. There was Southern fried chicken, just like every Sunday, and ham and roast beef. There were homemade biscuits, huge bowls of potato salad, and plates of deviled eggs, and from my uncles' gardens, fresh green beans, corn on the cob, and an assortment of fresh raw vegetables. Each of the women baked her own specialty cake or pie for dessert, and on this occasion we also churned homemade ice cream. The children in the bunch took turns on the handle of the churn. At first, this was an honor. But soon, our shoulders would tire, and then hurt, and we were glad to give way to the next hero. That ice cream tasted better than any since, and I can still feel the ice cream headache I got when I ate it too quickly.

After we ate, the women cleaned and the men sat on the porch, chatting. Their usual topics were the weather and sports, but most of what I overheard that day was about my mother, my sisters, and me, the rough times we'd had, and our prospects for the future. I didn't hang around to listen beyond that—I had too much exploring to catch up on. Behind my aunt's house were woods with a creek running through. Those woods had always been our favorite place to play. They lent themselves naturally to our favorite game: Tarzan. I was the biggest boy so I got to be Tarzan, even though my little sister could do the yell better than I could. Unfortunately for her, she was the smallest of us all, so she had to be Cheetah. We wore ourselves out running, jumping, climbing trees, and wading through the creek.

After we got too tired to run and climb trees, we went hunting for wild plums and blackberries. In spite of all the food we'd eaten earlier, we still found room for these natural delicacies. I wolfed down so many plums I got a bellyache. But that passed quickly, and I even tried a few of the blackberries the girls had found.

By the time twilight drew near, we headed back to the house, guided by the lightning bugs that never ceased to amaze us with their flickering lights.

As we neared the house, we could see the adults sitting on the porch. All my aunts and uncles were gathered around my mother. When we got close enough to hear their conversation, my aunt said, "At least, you're all back together again." When Mother looked up at us kids coming back into the yard there were tears streaming down her cheeks.

The day ended like all such days when children are involved. We were worn out and lethargic and had to be lifted into the back seat of the car for the trip home to our basement apartment. That worn-out feeling lasted for a couple of days and became a part of the memory of the occasion. This particular gathering, which truly marked a new beginning for my family, lingers warm and misty, after all this time. ⟋ઌ

The Four O'Clock Ritual

by Shannon Rulé | *Natchez, Mississippi*

IT WAS SUNDAY AFTERNOON, just after four o'clock, and everyone was arriving at Grandma's house. Grandma had a tiny little house that sat on a bluff at the edge of the highway in Natchez, Mississippi. It was white with fire-engine-red trim, and a long front porch that stretched from end to end. All the aunts and uncles settled themselves into rocking chairs while other kinfolk dragged kitchen chairs outside, packing more relatives onto the narrow porch.

Looking back on it now, a red-and-white house seems eccentric. But it didn't back then. It was just my grandma's house. I loved riding down the highway and seeing the house from a distance. I loved the first glimpse as much as I hated leaving and watching the red and white fade from my vision as I leaned on the back of the car seat and stared out of the rear window.

My family lived a ways from Natchez, but we made it for Sunday afternoon coffee as often as we could. Because Grandma lived on a divided highway, when we left, we had to loop around and pass back by the house. Each time we made that loop, Daddy pressed the horn long and hard. I waved my head off as aunts, uncles, and cousins hung off the porch, waving goodbye. I will always remember the sound of Daddy honking that horn. It was a ritual, like a long hug goodbye.

Grandma had ten or eleven children—no one could quite remember which. It depended on whether you counted the ones who had just moved in. Momma said that people back then did things like that. What was one more mouth to feed if you already had ten or eleven?

Now that her children were all grown with a new crop of young 'uns, myself included, plenty of people showed up at four o'clock for Sunday coffee. Grandma expected it. I heard that if you lived in Natchez and didn't show up on Sunday afternoon, come Monday morning you could expect a call. Grandma wanted to know who was sick enough to miss Sunday coffee.

I had lots of cousins, and we spent some magical times playing at Grandma's house. In the side yard, Grandma had a humongous cane patch that grew as tall as a man and as thick as weeds. We spent hours in that cane jungle, hiding and thrashing about. Now, whenever I see a cane patch, I think of Grandma's house and playing with all of my cousins.

Inside the house, a big spread of desserts always covered the kitchen table. One yellow pound cake had a special sweet sauce, which you spooned over the top. Every woman there, at her husband's urging, tried to discover Grandma's recipe for that sweet sauce, but when asked, Grandma confessed that she didn't have a recipe. She had learned by watching her own mother long years before. Hoping to learn her secrets, some of the aunts watched Grandma stir the sauce carefully to perfection. They later admitted that their sauce was just never as good as hers.

Then there was the big chocolate cake Grandma always made. I've never seen a cake like that since. The chocolate icing was thin but very hard. She pressed pecan halves all over the cake, about an inch apart. I remember the Sunday my brother Skip and I went into the deserted kitchen, gingerly lifted the cake cover, and proceeded to pull all the pecans off the cake and eat them. Can you imagine Grandma's face when she lifted the heavy metal cake cover and saw her chocolate cake with holes like polka dots where pecans had been? I don't remember her ever saying a word to us, but I'm sure she knew who the culprits were.

After Grandma passed on, the little white house with the red trim was sold, and few aunts and uncles gathered at four o'clock for Sunday afternoon coffee anymore. At my house, though, I noticed that my own mother would start filling the coffee pot about four o'clock in the afternoon. As I got older, we shared our own four o'clock coffee ritual.

Eventually, I moved away and had my own home. Every day at about four o'clock I would get the greatest urge for a cup of coffee. It was almost like I could smell it brewing before I even got the coffee filters out.

Later, I moved back to be near my mother, and every afternoon there was an unspoken invitation to four o'clock coffee. I would pull into her driveway and smile, knowing the minute I reached the front door I'd smell the deep, unmistakable aroma of coffee brewing.

Though my mother is gone now, the ritual is not. Even today, I could set my watch by that undiminished urge that comes about four o'clock, linking generations together by a family ritual begun on the front porch of a tiny little house that sat on a bluff, at the edge of a highway, in Natchez, Mississippi.

The Best Gift of All

by Michael L. Harvey | *Walhalla, North Dakota*

IT MUST HAVE BEEN SOMETIME IN THE LATE 1940S when several families gathered for the holidays at the home of James and Mabel Mathison. Their farm was south of Walhalla, North Dakota, across the county road from James's parents. In addition to the families of John and Minnie Mathison, some of Mabel's family from the Arneson side showed up, as well as Rachel Halverson, Grandma to everyone.

Most holidays found this mixture of families. Aunts, uncles, cousins, in-laws, and cousins-once-removed all enjoyed being with each other, regardless of the lack of formal family links. Different holidays found us at different homes with different blends of family members. The friendship, warmth, and love we shared never changed.

The kids ate in the kitchen filled with the smells of baking, roasting, and frying, as the mother of each family brought her specialty. Families who lived close by brought meat or foods that spoiled easily. Families traveling a distance always came with food that traveled well. My mom worked as a bookkeeper in a bakery, so we always came with bread. But Grandma's rolls tasted best.

Our gatherings were truly peaceful, and no matter whose house was home to the event, each was a welcoming place of love and safety.

At one particular meeting, my cousin Arden and I, both about ten years old, were impatient for the holiday meal to end. The farmyard was full of snowdrifts waiting to be tunneled, made into snowballs, and slid on with sleds and pieces of cardboard. Finally, the meal was over, and kids old enough to walk were bundled up and released into the outdoors like prisoners at the end of a long sentence. While the younger kids slid down the drifts in the side yard, Arden and I led older kids in digging out tunnels in the backyard drifts.

The frigid North Dakota winter soon made everyone cold, wet, shivery, red cheeked, and happy to come back inside. The pile of wet, soggy clothes was immense. Damp clothes were draped over wooden clothes racks, chair backs, and broom handles placed over chairs. Clothes that actually dripped water were banished to the entry shed, and everyone was given a change of warm, dry clothes.

As I added my bundle to the pile, I noticed Grandma standing at the door to the downstairs bedroom, a look of pure contentment on her face. Grandma and I had always enjoyed a special bond. At my difficult birth, doctors feared I would not live long, but Grandma held me, comforted me, fed me my mother's milk from an eyedropper, and did not let death win.

When Grandma saw me standing there watching her, she held a finger to her lips to tell me to be quiet. Softly, she called "Michael Lee, come quiet."

She slowly opened the door. The bed was ringed with pillows, quilts, blankets, and grownup's coats. The middle of the bed was filled with babies and small children all fast asleep.

I looked, but I don't think we saw the same thing. What I saw was only a bunch of drooling, smelly kids—too young to play with. But, now, as a grandparent, I see through Grandma's shining eyes and what I see is a bed full of promise, and hopes and dreams, and the future, and the best present God can give. Today, I thank Grandma for letting me look, even if it took me over forty years to see. ๑๖

The Lamp's Still Burning

by Charlene A. Derby (as told by Deborah Lombard) | *Bronson, Michigan*

"How's THAT REMODEL COMING?" my coworker, Sheila, asked as I clocked out at work. "Is it time to plan the housewarming party?"

"Not just yet," I replied, "but we're getting there. Rough electrical is in and drywall is next. I can't wait to see what the crew did today."

"Have a good evening," Sheila called as I headed for my car. On the thirty-minute drive home I had plenty of time to reflect on the project that's consumed my time and energy for the past three years.

Each day sheds new light on family history. Sometimes, I still can't believe that the American foursquare that's been in our family for four generations is now mine. The house, the foundation of our family, the one constant that has been a part of all of our gatherings—both happy and sad—had been placed in my hands for safekeeping.

"I want you to have the house," Mom had said when she was planning her will. "The other girls can have the money." As a single mother with a teenaged son, I understood and appreciated what she meant. She wouldn't be around to help in any other way, and she wanted me and Ray to have a good home.

That the house needed major repair became evident within a year of moving in. The decision to keep the lights on in my ancestral home didn't come easily. Because of my modest income, I considered selling it to a local camp for use as a retreat center. A nephew also expressed interest. After deliberating the sell/keep decision, I decided to keep the old homestead and asked one of my sisters to help me get a home equity loan.

Working with a local contracting company, we made plans for the remodel. The original electrical system, installed by Great Uncle Floyd in the 1930s, couldn't handle modern appliances. The plumbing installed by Dad in the 1960s couldn't handle a garbage disposal. The space heater that replaced Grandma's wood-burning stove couldn't keep the rooms warm enough. This time around, we'd do a thorough job—new electrical, new plumbing, new heating.

"Thorough" would mean stripping the interior down to the studs. But before we could begin the project, I had to clear out the house. Not wanting to waste any time, Ray and I moved into a nearby trailer and began the task of emptying the house.

Sending my sisters' high school trinkets to them was the easy part. It got harder once I started on the attic and garret. Nothing had been moved in these rooms for nearly fifty years. Many squirrel-chewed schoolbooks were thrown out. Some "junk" went to auction, and some parts of family heirlooms were stored in plastic bins in the basement. Of special interest was the brass bowl for an Aladdin oil lamp I'd found in the garret. Great Uncle Floyd had wired one of Grandmother's Aladdin lamps with a Jadeite bowl for electricity, and I wanted to convert this brass bowl into an electrical lamp similar to Grandmother's.

One day, as the construction shift ended, Bill, a crew member and distant cousin, came by the trailer to drop off a hook, which had once been used to button a woman's high top shoe.

"We found this between the studs" he explained.

I added it to my pile of "finds," which included a handful of fountain pen nibs and frames from a pair of wire-rimmed glasses. Then I showed him the Aladdin lamp bowl I'd discovered.

I rubbed the lamp and smiled. "I want to turn this into an electrical lamp, but I don't have a mantle to go with it."

Bill shrugged. "I bet we could find a mantle on the Internet. If you'd like, I can help you search."

I sat down next to him at the computer as he brought up the search engine. Soon, we were scrolling through pages of lamps, mantles, and replacement parts.

"I have those!" I squealed as we viewed a set of wires for holding the mantle.

I pointed to the picture on the screen. "Ray, see if you can find these over at the house." In a short while, Ray returned with the wires. The "tripod," as it was called, fit my bowl perfectly!

With a little more searching, both on the Internet and through the construction site, we discovered I had all of the parts of an original Aladdin lamp, except for the mantle. By the end of the evening, Bill and I were almost dancing around the computer. "I've got my lamp!" I exclaimed. "I can't believe it!"

When the mantle arrived, I used the individual pieces and created a complete oil-burning Aladdin lamp. I liked the idea of having an original family flame as part of my new decor. It was one of the first finished projects of the remodel and meant a great deal to both me and Ray.

As I drove toward home after my shift at work, I saw the house on a slight rise about a half mile ahead, a cherry-blossom sunset reflected in its windows. Beyond the house, a light in the trailer made it easy to see my son moving around inside. Optimistically, I wondered if Ray had finished his shift at the pizzeria early and had already started dinner.

I pulled into the driveway and park beside Ray's battered excuse for a first car. "What's cooking?" I asked as I entered through the kitchen door.

"What? Me cook?" Ray joked. He held up the pizza box. "I got your favorite pizza."

I noticed that he'd set the table, using the Aladdin lamp as the centerpiece.

"Hey, Mom," Ray said, as he sat down at the table. "Let's keep the house. I'm a country boy, you know."

"Of course we'll keep it. Why do you think we've worked so hard over the past three years?" Inside, I was grinning, pleased that he wanted to stay. "You'll have to share, though."

"Say what?" Ray looked surprised.

I glanced out the window at the house and then back at my son. In his face, I saw my ancestors—my grandfather, my grandmother—and I remembered the family gatherings of old, and wished with all of my heart to duplicate them. "I want my sisters and their families to think of the house as their place in the country, too. Now that the squirrels have been evicted from the attic, there's plenty of room for everyone."

A slow smile crossed Ray's face and he nodded toward the center of the table. I saw a newfound maturity shining in his eyes, and my throat caught on his next words.

"Yeah," he agreed. "Let's light the lamp for them." ᧁ

Contributors

Trish Ayers ("Never Say No to Nina"), a twenty-year resident of Berea, Kentucky, has been writing since she could hold a pencil. Working on essays, poetry, short stories, novels, and especially plays has become a healing salve for her while facing a chronic illness. Her dramatic works have been produced and staged across the country, in Kentucky, Seattle, Pennsylvania, and in Japan.

David L. Barber ("Grandma's Roses") has been writing poetry and short stories for over twenty-five years, from locations around the world, as a member of the air force. He is now retired and works in Albuquerque, New Mexico. He has recently had three poems published in the online magazine *www.peopleofthebible.com, Indite Circle magazine,* and on *www.kavitanjali.com.* David, who is also an artist and a musician, is working on a novel entitled *E-Planet.*

Barbara Beaudoin ("A Little Piano Music") uses her stories to record and share memories and family history with five children and six grandchildren. She and her husband have recently moved into a new condominium complex to allow them more time for travel and hobbies—her writing and painting, and his wood-crafting.

N. V. Bennett ("Wishbone Science") lives and writes from Vancouver Island. Her work can also be seen in various inspirational anthologies, including *A Cup of Comfort for Sisters*, and in magazines like *Young Rider, Lake Country Journal, Presbyterian Today, The Christian Science Monitor, The Anglican Journal, Woman of Spirit, Glad Tidings,* and *Messenger of the Sacred Heart.* She raises very small chickens and reads them recipes when they are lax in their laying.

Lanita Bradley Boyd ("Perfect Pitch") draws on her life experiences to inspire others into a closer relationship with God. She is the founder of the Sisterhood of Christian Writers, a national coalition of woman writers. Lanita has been published in various anthologies and periodicals. She can be reached through her Web site, at *www.lanitaboyd.com*.

John R. Bradley ("Clearview Christmas") is an attorney in Sumner County, Tennessee. He has been the city attorney for Hendersonville since 1987. His aunt, Lola Mae Bradley Empson, is retired after forty years of teaching Sumner County students. Lola Mae, John, and John's mother, Mary Ralph Bradley ("A Jaunt to Aunt Josie's"), are part of the story "Perfect Pitch," which is also in this anthology.

Mary Ralph Bradley ("A Jaunt to Aunt Josie's") has been a teacher, Gallup pollster, and operator of a bed-and-breakfast. Presently, she is a law-office manager, farmer, and school-board member, and above all, a believer in Jesus Christ. She is the author of *Memories, Mysteries, and Musings* and has stories in various anthologies. Her Tennessee home, Ajalon Acres, is a haven for the downtrodden—some for hours, others for years.

Barbara Brady ("Cousin Jean"), a retired registered nurse, lives in Topeka, Kansas, with her husband of almost fifty years. She enjoys church, sunflowers, books, volunteer activities, and most of all her family and friends. Barbara is the author of *A Variety of Gifts, Smiling at the Future,* and *Seasoned with Salt.* Her work has been published in various markets.

LB Brumage ("A Sure Thing") was born and raised in West Virginia. She now lives with her family in the Midwest. LB is a fiction/essay writer and executive editor for a leading publisher of tax and business law information.

Renie Burghardt ("The Uninvited Visitor"), was born in Hungary, and is a freelance writer with many credits. She has contributed to various inspirational anthologies, a dozen *Guideposts* books, and many others. She lives in the country and loves nature, animals, gardening, reading, and spending time with family and friends.

Carol Burnside ("Homecoming") currently is a full-time writer and member of Romance Writers of America, with several works submitted to various commercial publications.

Lucile C. Cason ("Swamp Family") enjoys writing poetry and creative nonfiction. A registered nurse for more years than she cares to admit, she is currently writing a novel (labeled fiction to make it believable) about human reactions to traumatic life-changing events, including her own. She is a graduate of Emory University in Atlanta, Georgia.

Rita Chandler ("Unfailing Love"), writing under a pseudonym, has had work published in *The Rocking Chair Reader*'s flagship book, *Coming Home*, and in various devotional magazines. Rita was a secretary in Southern California, where she lived for more than forty years.

Lisa Ciriello ("A Recipe for Success") is a freelance writer and baker. She lives in Warwick, New York, with her husband and pets.

Joan Clayton ("Things Money Cannot Buy") is a retired educator who also has been the religion columnist for her local newspaper for eleven years. She has written eight books and has had over 500 articles published. Joan has appeared three times in *Who's Who Among America's Teachers* and was Woman of the Year 2003 in her town of Portales, New Mexico. She has been married to the love of her life for fifty-six years, and she has three sons and six grandchildren.

Jean Davidson ("The Bunny of Easters Past") resides in Pocatello, Idaho. She is a "junior" senior at Idaho State University. Her studies target whatever piques her interest, from metal jewelry making, to Egyptian studies, to political science. Jean's greatest pleasures, however, are in being part of a great family whose stories she loves to write. She is currently working on a family cookbook and a historical novel based upon women of the Old West.

Charlene A. Derby ("The Lamp's Still Burning") lives in Southern California with her husband and son. Her stories have appeared in several compilation books as well as in *Reminisce Extra* and *Focus on the Family* magazines. She is the proud owner of Grandma's Jadeite Aladdin lamp.

Sam E. Douglas ("The Family Together"), a retired military man, served in air force intelligence all over the world, including during the Vietnam War. He has a B.S. degree from the University of Maryland and an M.S. from Webster University. Currently, Samuel is a freelance writer living in South Carolina with his wife of over forty-five years. They have two sons. One is in law enforcement in the Baltimore area, and the other is a magazine editor/writer in New York City. His work has appeared in various university, small press, and online publications.

Betty Downs ("Then There Were Six" and "Aunt Clara's Tears") was raised on the prairies of North Dakota but has called the Black Hills of South Dakota home for the past fifty years, forty of which were spent moving through four states with her construction-roving husband. Now widowed, Betty is enjoying gardening and traveling, and is delighted to be published in *The Upper Room, Reminisce, A Cup of Comfort*, and the anthology, *Crazy Woman Creek*. She has four sons and seven grandchildren who keep life interesting.

Sandy Williams Driver ("A Southern Family Reunion") and her husband Tim live in Albertville, Alabama, where both were born and raised. They have three children: Josh, Jake, and Katie. Sandy has been a full-time writer for three years. Her stories have been included in several magazines, newspapers, and anthologies, including *The Rocking Chair Reader: Coming Home.*

T. Suzanne Eller ("One of the Family") is an author and speaker. She and Richard, her husband of twenty-five years, live happily in Oklahoma. Suzanne can be reached by e-mail at *tseller@daretobelieve.org.*

Margaret A. Frey ("Dinner at Dora's") started her career as a copy/production editor in Philadelphia, Pennsylvania. Her fiction and nonfiction have appeared in print and online including: *Writer's Digest, Christian Science Monitor, Futures Anthology, Literary Potpourri, Smokelong Quarterly, Wild Strawberries*, and elsewhere. Future work will appear in *Mindprints Literary Journal*. Margaret writes from the foothills of the Smoky Mountains where she lives with her husband, and canine literary critic Ruffian.

Geoffrey Girard ("The Twelve-Year Bog") was raised in New Jersey and is currently an English teacher in Ohio. Girard's work has recently appeared in *Writers of the Future XIX*. His novel, *Tales of the Jersey Devil*, was published by Middle Atlantic Press, October 2004.

Lynn R. Hartz ("The Best Present") lives in Charleston, West Virginia. Her stories have appeared in *A Cup of Comfort for Christmas* and *Small Miracles for Families*. She has authored three books: *And Time Stood Still*, the story of the midwife who delivered the Christ Child; *Club Fed: Living in a Women's Prison*; and *Praise Him in Prison*.

Michael L. Harvey ("The Best Gift of All") is a semiretired computer programmer from North Dakota. Harvey was raised in an extended family of parents, grandparents, and cousins. He has had humorous essays published in the *Midnight Zoo* magazine and articles published in the local newspaper. For over twenty years, Michael has enjoyed collecting, and telling and writing family stories.

Nancy Jackson ("A Need for Independence") grew up in Oregon and moved to the coast in her twenties. The Fourth of July parade, a time when everyone forgot their personal problems and came together, was almost her favorite aspect of living in Gleneden Beach. She wished there had been more than just one Fourth of July a year. Today, Nancy is a mother and has shared the experience with her son as well.

Rachel J. Johnson ("Apple Butter Day") writes poetry, children's stories, and narratives. She also teaches English as a second language, tutors online, and home schools her two daughters. Rachel loves to read, explore nature, and train for marathons. She lives with her husband and children in Kansas City, Missouri. Visit her Web site at *www.wakeuprunning.com*.

Carol Kehlmeier ("The Wondrous Seashell") is a former newspaper-woman and columnist. Today, Carol is an active freelance writer in Westerville, Ohio. She is a wife, mother, and grandmother. She enjoys listening to music, family get-togethers, and walks in the woods.

Candy Killion ("A Pear in the Sand"), a freelance writer living near Fort Lauderdale, Florida, lived in New Jersey for more than four decades—each move bringing her a little bit closer to the beach. Her work has appeared in numerous newspapers, magazines, greeting cards, and the Internet, as well as in the *They Lied!* humor anthology series.

Betty R. Koffman ("The Gathering Place"), a native of Kentucky, grew up in eastern Tennessee in the foothills of the Smoky Mountains. She has a degree in English from East Tennessee State University, and she lives and writes in Kingsport.

Kristin Dreyer Kramer ("Home on the Lake") is the editor-in-chief of the Web site *www.NightsAndWeekends.com*. You can find her online, or in a lounge chair on the beach at the cottage.

Suzanne LaFetra ("From Grave to Cradle") is an award-winning writer who lives with her family in Northern California. She is currently at work on a novel and a children's book.

Emmarie Lehnick ("Mama's Birthday"), of Amarillo, Texas, is a retired teacher with a B.S. and M.A. in English/Speech. She is a member of Inspirational Writers Alive, and has been published in magazines and two volumes of *A Cup of Comfort*. She and her husband have a daughter, son, and four grandsons.

Elaine Young McGuire ("Tennessee Celebrations"), a retired teacher, writes articles and devotionals from her home in Lilburn, Georgia. She has been published in many periodicals, including *Upper Room* and *Angels on Earth*. Elaine has signed contracts for several stories to appear in upcoming anthologies.

Jacquie McTaggart ("Saturday Night on the Town") began work as a freelance writer, following a forty-two-year teaching career. She currently writes weekly columns on education and parenting issues for two metropolitan Iowa newspapers. Several of her articles have been published in national magazines and on the Internet. Her book, *From the Teacher's Desk*, was released in December 2003. Today, she travels throughout the country keynoting at state reading conferences and serving as guest instructor to aspiring teachers. She and her husband, Carroll, live in Iowa. They have two sons and six grandkids—including a set of twins.

Pat Capps Mehaffey ("Little Boy Lost"), an ex-banker, retired to a lake cabin where she enjoys birds, grandchildren, and writing. From the serenity of this location, Pat wrote and published two Christian meditation books— with a third near completion. She also has had several stories accepted in *The Rocking Chair Reader* series, as well as the *Cup of Comfort* series of books. One of Pat's stories was recently published in *The Noble Generation II* and in 2003 she won first place in a regional obituary-writing contest.

Alice A. Mendelsohn ("The Screen House") has written poetry since she was a little girl. She is a member of Women Who Write and has discovered the enjoyment of creative nonfiction and personal essays. In recent years, Alice was privileged to have a byline column in a local newspaper and more recently has had poems appear in local publications.

Michelle Close Mills ("Wilbur's Vanishing Act") is originally from Ft. Wayne, Indiana, but she currently resides in Florida with her husband Ralph. "Wilbur's Vanishing Act" is only one of the many childhood memories tape-recorded by her late grandmother Helen Clay-Sprague. Michelle has written for various newspapers and poetry publications.

E. Dian Moore ("The Elves Under the Stairs") is a Christian freelance writer and editor living in the northern panhandle of West Virginia. She maintains a Web site for writers, and her hands are the hands behind *www.handsforhope.com*. Moore began writing in high school, fell in love with the creative process, and lived for writing assignments, much to the dismay of her classmates.

Lad Moore ("The Prayer Wheel"), a former corporate executive, has returned to his roots in East Texas. His writings have been published more than 400 times in print and on the Internet, including two short story collections through BeWrite Books. He has received several writing awards and credits, which include appearances in *Carolina Country, Amarillo Bay,*

Pittsburgh Quarterly, and in various anthologies. Visit Lad's Web site at *http://ladmoore.homestead.com/home.html.*

Amy M. O'Quinn ("Silvertone Memories") is married to a Primitive Baptist preacher. A former schoolteacher, Amy now homeschools her five children. Her writing background includes stories and articles published in several magazines, including *GEORGIA Magazine, Guideposts for Kids, Jack and Jill, International Gymnast,* and *Classic Education's Learning Through History Magazine.*

Sharon Cupp Pennington ("A Wee Gathering") resides in Texas and is presently working on her first romantic suspense novel, *Hoodoo Money.* Her short stories have been published in *The Emporium Gazette, The Written Wisdom, Seasons for Writing, FlashQuake, Mocha Memoirs,* and *Flash Shots.*

Linda Kaullen Perkins ("Christmas at Napoleon"), freelance writer and novelist, has had articles published in several local newspapers and currently contributes a monthly selection of short stories to *Party Line,* a local magazine. After retiring in 2001 after thirty-one years as an elementary teacher, Linda completed a 70,000-word historical manuscript. She is a member of Romance Writers of America and a weekly critique group.

Kim Peterson ("Where I Belong") serves as writer-in-residence at Bethel College in Mishawaka, Indiana. Her articles have appeared in various anthologies and magazines, including *AppleSeeds* children's magazine, *Encounter* magazine, *Elkhart (IN) Truth,* and a variety of Sunday school take-home papers.

Rachael Phillips ("Dixie Pool") has published four popular biographies (*Frederick Douglass, Billy Sunday, St. Augustine,* and a collection of four mini-biographies of Christian hymn writers), as well as several humorous magazine articles. She has won several awards, including the 2004 Erma Bombeck Global Award for humor. Rachael and her husband Steve, the parents of three grown children, enjoy their life in the small town of Plymouth, Indiana.

Cheryl K. Pierson ("The Sugar-Cube Cure") lives in Oklahoma City with her husband and two children. Cheryl, a freelance writer and novelist, currently is working on her third romance novel. She is co-owner of FabKat Editorial Services (*www.westwindsmedia.com*), where she teaches workshops and weekly writing classes as well as edits manuscripts for other authors.

Anna M. Popescu ("Sisters on Vacation") is the author of the Christian contemporary novel, *A Little Bit of Wonderful*, and has had articles published in *Light and Life, The Front Porch, HopeKeepers, Spirit-Led Writer, Home Cooking, The Family Beat, Joy & Praise, The Gem*, and *This Christian Life*, as well as in book anthologies. Her devotionals appear online. She and her husband Rick live in northern Arizona with their Sheltie named Bleu.

Penny Porter ("My Chair"), married to Bill Porter, a retired cattle rancher, is the mother of six, grandmother of eight, and great-grandmother of one. She has always been in love with life and family. Penny, the author of five books, currently is president of the Society of Southwestern Authors. Her work has been published in a wide range of magazines, including *Reader's Digest, Arizona Highways, Guideposts, Catholic Digest*, and several anthologies, including *The Rocking Chair Reader*.

Dorothy Read ("Buses, Trains, and Taxicabs") is a retired English teacher who lives on Whidbey Island, near Seattle. She sees stories springing from every situation, present and past. She shares, in this volume, her personal memories of being a child during World War II. Her stories have appeared in three anthologies.

Roberta Rhodes ("The Windswept Prairie") grew up in Cheyenne, Wyoming, and now resides in Erie, Pennsylvania. She attended Edinboro University in Pennsylvania and currently writes a monthly column for an area newspaper. Roberta has been published in several national magazines.

Virginia Rowledge ("Summer's Dance") grew up in hilly Connecticut country with lots of time to read and appreciate sky, clouds, and wildflowers. She graduated in 1953, and moved to Florida in 1971, where she is a hearing instrument specialist. Virginia finds it gratifying to help people to hear the sounds of life. Writing is her passion.

Marcia Rudoff ("Summertime") is a retired educator. She lives in Bainbridge Island, Washington, where she writes a column for *The Bainbridge Review* and teaches memoir writing to senior citizens. Marcia enjoys walking, volunteering, reading, writing, and visiting with children, grandchildren, and siblings and friends. Also high on her priority list are baseball, chocolate, and getting published.

Shannon Rulé ("The Four O'Clock Ritual") is a freelance writer and paralegal. Having grown up in the Mississippi delta, her storytelling is as rich as the soil she thrived in. She favors inspirational, memoir, and humor writing.

Al Serradell ("Welcome to the Family"), a Los Angeles native, is a veteran writing instructor in the Oklahoma City area. A professional journalist, he has worked for newspapers in Oklahoma (the *Journal Record*, the *Guthrie News Leader*) and Colorado (the *Rocky Mountain News*), and co-owns an editorial business, FabKat Editorial Services (*www.westwindsmedia.com*).

Susan G. Sharp-Anderson ("In Search of a Christmas Tree") was born in Hawaii but reared in Los Angeles. Susan spent twenty years in Oregon raising her three children and currently lives in St. Thomas, in the Virgin Islands, and Williamsport, Pennsylvania, working as a forensic dentist and deputy coroner, as well as managing portions of her family-run corporation.

Jan Sparkman ("The Visit") is the author of a novel, three books of nonfiction, several short stories and articles, and hundreds of newspaper columns. Her short story collection, *Silk and Steel: Stories of Strong Women*, will be published in the spring of 2005. Jan has a B.A. in Writing and Literature from Burlington College, Burlington, Vermont, and currently serves on the board of the Laurel County Historical Society and the Janice Holt Giles and Henry Giles Society. She lives in London, Kentucky, with her husband of forty-six years and has three grown children and seven grandchildren.

Mary Helen Straker ("Hearthstone Halloween"), formerly a newspaper and magazine reporter, has had her work published in the form of both short fiction and nonfiction, and has had two short stories published in the

A Cup of Comfort series. She currently is working on a family memoir and has led a workshop in memoir-writing at a Columbus, Ohio, library.

Lucinda Rickett Strine ("Threshing Adventures on the Farm") retired in 1992, after thirty-two years as a public school teacher. She has been a freelance writer since 1976. With the support of the Mt. Eaton Historical Society, she authored a 121-page book, *Paint Township Mt. Eaton, Ohio*, in 2003, for Ohio's Bicentennial. Lucinda enjoys writing about her happy childhood on the farm homestead outside of the tiny village of Nova, Ohio.

Gayle Sorensen Stringer ("Farmhouse") is a teacher and freelance writer. She enjoyed her childhood on a dairy farm near the small, southwestern Minnesota community of Tyler. After years of living in various urban communities, she has recently relocated with her husband and three children to the small, rural town of Abingdon, Virginia. Happily, she once again breathes fresh, country air and walks among cows.

David Crane Swarts ("Honest Question, Honest Answer") received his education at Rushville Consolidated High School, and received his BSME at Duke University. He is a registered professional engineer (PE) in Illinois and Indiana, and lived in the Chicago, Illinois, area from 1972 to 1996. He returned to Fort Wayne, Indiana, in 1996. He is the father of two sons, Zachary, eight, and Daniel, five.

James E. Tate ("Homemade Ice Cream at Grandma's") has had his work published in various publications, including *The Saturday Evening Post, Route 66 Magazine*, and *Word Aflame*. Since retiring from Southwestern Bell Telephone Company, he writes three poetry columns regularly. He and his wife, Marie, live in Tulsa, Oklahoma. They raised three children and have five grandchildren, who have blessed them with thirteen great-grandchildren.

Avis A. Townsend ("Scents of Remembrance") is an award-winning author. Avie, who has been writing for over twenty years, has one published novel. Her work can be found in many anthologies and on her Web site *www.avietownsend.com*.

Ray Weaver ("The Crab Feast") is a published singer/songwriter. Originally from the United States, Ray now lives and works in Denmark.

Garnet Hunt White ("As the Wedding March Played") is a retired schoolteacher. She lives outside the Doniphan, Missouri, city limits. Garnet loves animals and takes care of stray dogs and cats. Her work has been published in a variety of publications, including *The Rocking Chair Reader: Coming Home*.

Patricia Wilson ("Grandmother's Imagination") is a dental hygienist, but her grandmother's music has been her passion for many years. She produced the CD *Songs from Grandmother's House* and wrote the children's book *I Can't See, But I Can Imagine* including a CD with the story and five of her grandmother's songs.

Margaret Anne Wright ("Watermelon Preserves") was born and raised in Peterborough, Ontario. She graduated from York University with a bachelor's degree in English. Margaret wrote "Independent at Heart," which was published in the anthology *Single Women: Alive and Well*.

Kristine Ziemnik ("The Memory Boxes" and "A Few Minutes Ago") lives with her husband, Joseph, in lovely, historic Chippewa Lake, Ohio. She owns a home-based craft business called Kristine's Kreations. Writing stories is another of her creative outlets, and she plans to write a book someday.

Kimberly Zweygardt ("Getting Up with the Sun") is married to the love of her life, Kary. Together they are active in the community and church in Saint Francis, Kansas. They have three children, Jordan, Lauren, and Britt, and a menagerie that includes two black Labs, Lucy and Dozer, a double-dapple dachshund named Inky-Dinky-Doodles, Clifford, the big red cat, a fish named Phish, and two frogs. Kim enjoys writing, performing dramatic interpretations, cooking, and travel. Visit her at *www.kimzweygardt.com*.

About the Editor

HELEN KAY POLASKI has always believed in magic, especially the kind that keeps marriages together, binds siblings and friends, and ties the concept of home close to the heart. She is the seventh child in a family of sixteen children—eleven sisters and four brothers—and has more nieces, nephews, and cousins than she can count. Helen hails from Metz, Michigan, a small town just 60 miles southeast of the Mackinac Bridge. She married her high school sweetheart, Thomas, who is number three in a family of nine. They have been married for twenty-nine years and have three children: April, Alissa, and Nathan. After seventeen years as a newspaper reporter/photographer and editor, Helen left her full-time job to follow her dream of becoming a book author. In the past four years, she has worn many hats, including book author, book editor, storyteller, essayist, journalist, poet, book and movie reviewer, songwriter, and co-president of the Southeast Michigan Writers' Association. When not on the computer, she is busy exploring the world with her family, and is pleased to say most trips still take her back home where the magic is strongest.